In The Spirit Of Black Elk:
Preserving A Sacred Way

Torrey James Lystra
Red Hawk Books LLC

In The Spirit of Black Elk: Preserving A Sacred Way
Published in 2013 by Red Hawk Books LLC
Copyright c 2013 by Torrey James Lystra
All rights reserved.
Printed in the USA

No part of this book may be used or reproduced in any manner whatsoever without written permission except in the case of brief quotations embodied in critical articles and reviews. For information contact: redhawkbooks@gmail.com

Paintings and photographs by Torrey James Lystra
For more information on his art go to: torreylystra.com

The Library of Congress has catalogued this edition as follows:
Lystra, Torrey James, 1952
In The Spirit Of Black Elk: Preserving A Sacred Way
ISBN: 0989285103
ISBN 13: 9780989285100
Library of Congress Control Number: 2013909823
Red Hawk Books, Gig Harbor, Washington
Pbk.

TABLE OF CONTENTS

Introduction vii

A Sacred Way xxix

Dedication xxxiii

Chapter 1 Beginnings 1

Chapter 2 Sacred Men And Women-Wichasa Wakans . 29

Chapter 3 Purification 49

Chapter 4 Ancient Traditions 57

Chapter 5 Singing A New Memory 67

Chapter 6 Wallace Black Elk Speaks 79

Chapter 7 Seven Sacred Fires 95

Chapter 8 In Two Worlds I Walk 113

Chapter 9 The Sacred Pipe-Chanunpa 127

Chapter 10 Spiritual Awakening 143

Chapter 11 Healing And Help 159

Chapter 12 Lakota Vision Quest-Hanbleycha 173

Chapter 13 Looking At The Sun They Dance 185

Chapter 14 Council With Eagles.................................... 203

Chapter 15 Stone Dreamers-Yuwipi............................... 217

Chapter 16 House Ceremony 225

Chapter 17 Medicine Stone.. 231

Chapter 18 Initiation... 239

Chapter 19 Ancient Mystery.. 265

Chapter 20 Red Hawk 273

Chapter 21 Black Elk Teachings:
Viejas Reservation... 281

Chapter 22 Angel Dialogue: California 293

Chapter 23 Bear Butte-Hanbleycha................................ 297

Chapter 24 Sacred Clowns-Heyoka Wichasas............... 305

Chapter 25 Shamanic Equilibrium 321

Chapter 26 Angel Dialogue: Washington State 331

Chapter 27 Orca Nation... 337

Chapter 28 Angel Dialogue: Orcas
Island, Washington 351

Epilogue... 357

INTRODUCTION

What would you do if a powerful shaman knocked on your door one day, and told you Spirit had directed him to teach you the principles and practices of an ancient lineage of sacred men and women? What would you do if he proved to you on many occasions that he had the ability to communicate with nature spirits, facilitate unusual healing and curing, see into your future or past, and at times affect the weather? Would you commit to the philosophy of his Sacred Way and practice those ways diligently during your lifetime?

What would you do if you met an angel face to face? How would you react if she explained that a life of peace, harmony, and happiness possibly awaited you in a distant unknown location? What would you do if she told you possible danger awaited you where you currently lived? Would you believe you actually had communicated with an angel? Would you take her advice if it meant leaving your present career, uprooting your family, and searching for the place she referred to with only the few clues she passed along?

I was faced with each of those questions over a quarter of a century ago. I am now sharing this information in this manner because I too have become a Grandfather. "In The Spirit Of Black Elk: Preserving A Sacred Way" offers the reader a unique look into my pathway of transformation on my way to becoming a "sacred man". It also serves as a way to honor those who have traversed this arduous trail before me. I have documented my experiences and those of my teachers in detail, to help preserve an ancient wisdom originally passed down orally in the age we refer to as prehistory. There were times when I felt I had entered a dangerous jungle pathway into the unknown.

Wallace Black Elk and his adopted son, Steve Red Buffalo, were my teachers in the beginning of this part of my story. One of Wallace Black Elk's teachers was the great Oglala sacred man, his adopted Grandfather, Nicholas Black Elk. He was a cousin to the renowned Crazy Horse. He was a friend to esteemed chiefs: Sitting Bull, Red Cloud, and American Horse. They had been instructed by revered *wichasa wakans*, "sacred men": Wirlwind Chaser, and Elk Head, who was the original keeper of the most powerful Sioux *Chanunpa Wakan*, "sacred pipe". Oral history records that a spirit called *Ptesan Win*, "White Buffalo Calf Woman", gave this sacred implement to the Lakota people many centuries ago. Wallace Black Elk explained to me that, "The sacred pipe is a device that we utilize to communicate with Spirit." The Chanunpa Wakan, associated with White Buffalo Calf Woman, is still in existence and is cared for as a holy relic by a chosen family within the Lakota nation. It remains a sacred connection to the healing, seeing, and being practices discussed here.

In the hands of one properly trained in its functions a Chanunpa can be a mind opening doorway into many possibilities, including non-ordinary realms where help can be sought to produce unusual healing and curing. My translations of Wallace Black Elk and Steve Red Buffalo's teaching and philosophy are a vital link to a long line of respected elders that extend into antiquity. The dialogue I share with my teachers during my apprenticeship offers a window into that lineage of respected sacred men and women.

Wallace Black Elk explained to me that he was chosen at the tender age of five years to carry the old ways into our modern world by eleven grandfathers and grandmothers. Those elders had determined that the ranks of the true wichasa wakans had been decimated by the pressures of the European invasion into their sacred lands, the deadly spread in epidemic proportions of unknown European diseases, and subsequent reservation internment. They felt that a knowledge-bearer in the new generation needed to be chosen and fully taught to help prevent their ancient path from ending with the few that were left.

A prophecy, nineteen generations previous, foretold that a little boy on the Rosebud Reservation would be instrumental in preserving the old ways for future generations. During a ceremony in which Wallace made his first contact with the spirits, it was indicated to the elders that he was the one to come. When his unprecedented extremely youthful apprenticeship began, spirit entities taught him many things including how to speak the English language, which he in turn helped his family to learn. He explained to me, "Grandson, I am uneducated regarding matters of formal schooling, however, my spirit helpers educate me regarding many levels of knowledge that I could acquire in no other manner." As you will read on these pages those nature spirits assisted him in many ways over many years. The main text of this book brings these intangible energies more clearly into focus.

My reporting in this document begins with my initial meeting of Wallace Black Elk and his wife Grace Spotted Eagle. Our meeting was orchestrated by Dr. William Lyon, an anthropologist who at that time was collecting data on Wallace Black Elk for a future book. The meeting took place at a park I helped design and manage for San Diego County Parks, an amazing wild canopy of oaks and sycamore trees in a canyon approximately one mile wide and two and a half miles long on a

584 acre ribbon along the western rim of Pauma Valley, California. I was 34 years of age, happily married, with my three young sons often by my side. I had received the Environmental Educator of the Year Award by the San Diego chapter of the Sierra Club and been named Interpreter of the Year and Ranger of the Year by San Diego County Parks, in previous seasons, for my teaching and design work at that facility.

At the time we met, Wallace Black Elk had faithfully carried the *Chanunpa Wakan* , of the Lakota (Oglala), for over half a century. He was one of the most widely known North American shamans, due mainly for his efforts to secure religious freedom for all traditional shamans here in the United States. We discussed the possibility of conducting several days of traditional teachings and ritual for those wishing the rare opportunity to experience one of man's oldest and direct forms of communication with nature. He told me he would speak about our real Mother the Earth, and how he uses her spirit guides in his daily life.

Grace Spotted Eagle, his wife, was going to contribute throughout the length of the teachings. She would speak about women and their powerful contributions to the well-being of our planet. Black Elk went on to describe a medicine wheel encampment where he and his assistants would guide us on a symbolic journey back to the womb of the Great Mother. "In the darkness of the *stone-people-lodge*, 'sweat lodge', we will support each other in search of that individual wisdom that underlies each of our beings-regardless of race or creed.

Wallace Black Elk began his teaching with me in our initial meeting. Over the years the majority of our time together was spent in that endeavor-with a great deal of laughter in between. To be perfectly clear, the term "apprentice" is rarely utilized by practicing sacred men or women who are sharing their knowledge in this manner . However, from the very beginning, he patiently gifted his philosophy and practices to me in the way a generous Grandfather would share with his Grandson. Dr. William Lyon commented to me, "Black Elk clearly plans to do some serious teaching with you." He pointed out that my Grandson designation was quite significant in the Native American manner of viewing family. He went on to explain that after traveling with Black Elk and Spotted Eagle for several years he was referred to as Nephew. Despite all the work he had done for them Dr. Lyon explained to me he was well aware that his own sacred instruction would be limited. Black Elk explained to me in our initial meeting that, "The spirits have directed me to you to share these sacred ways".

People sometimes ask me why a white skinned young family man, Grandson of a protestant minister, fully immersed in mainstream American life, was chosen to be a recipient of this ancient knowledge. I share with them what Grandfather Black Elk impressed upon me over and over, to not ask "why" about my circumstances. He felt asking "why" was to be trapped by a typical western response to reality. He explained that in order to move forward with his teaching I needed to set aside what I had learned to be the parameters of this reality to allow me to learn from my new experiences and awareness to form a more accurate reality. I had indeed been blessed with two very spiritual Grandfathers who each possessed a unique view of the cosmos. My Danish Grandfather, Janus Petersen, had his own view of the universe based on the authentic scriptural texts he studied throughout his protestant ministry. Bible stories of miraculous healing from my early upbringing made a lasting impression on me. I was twelve years of age when I left the dogma of that teaching behind through an unusual altercation that I describe later in this writing.   Grandfather Black Elk believed that a wichasa wakan was chosen while in their mothers' womb. And so I leave it at that.

I believe he knew I would not walk with the knowledge he passed along exactly as he had. However, I had to discover this for myself. He introduced me to other practicing shamans so I would receive a more complete view of the "sacred mystery powers". "We each walk with our powers in our own way", he stated. He told me the spirits themselves would teach me how to proceed during my work with him. He explained they would take over my teaching completely at some point in my future. My walk as a sacred man has continued through their guidance as he stated. "The power and the ways are given to a wichasa wakan to be passed on to others. The more power I give away, the more I receive, and if I do not share my gifts from the spirits to help others, I will lose them." His Grandfather Nicholas Black Elk shared the same sentiment with him and he wanted me to know it would be the same with me.

"Grandson, always remember that you must develop courage of the heart. The use of the Chanunpa and your ability to contact spirits through it depend on the purity of your consciousness. All pollution begins in the mind. And, you need patience-the ability to wait, and watch, and transcend time. Some things are worth waiting for. When you carry the Chanunpa everyone brings all their problems to you. You will need great endurance and strength to serve others this way. And you must develop alertness-learn to observe, to listen, and to remember. When these qualities have become strong in you, you will be walking a path of a humble man."

Wallace Black Elk shared his philosophy and practices with people of all skin colors, and he was sometimes criticized for this practice. However, he never let that criticism prevent him from his primary mandate of keeping these sacred ways alive. He emphasized to me, "Grandson, these ways belong to all people-not just the red nations. There was a time in the first age when all beings respected each other and they lived in harmony with the Earth Mother. The spirits say that is possible again in the next Great Age of mankind."

Over the course of my years of learning what I could from Black Elk and Red Buffalo there were many examples of paranormal phenomenon that solidified my place on this trail. Several of those experiences are revealed in this document. Each of those events furthered my own realization that I had been given a very special window into a sacred technology, and I applied my skills diligently to the tasks I was asked to accomplish.

My relationship with Grandfather was not perfect. His *heyoka medicine*, which I will define later in this text, created moody moments between us and at times I did not understand his actions regarding this area of the medicine he carried. However, his integrated sense of spirituality helped me understand that the gate to the sacred is found within our own bodies, hearts, and minds. He taught me I must begin within myself to discover my own place in the worlds of a shaman.

Though I came from humble beginnings I never faced the prejudice and extreme poverty that he overcame in his life. He was a highly intelligent, dedicated, humorous, humble man who exhibited great courage and kindness throughout our years together.

The beginning chapters of this book, document many of my early conversations with Steve Red Buffalo, Wallace Black Elk, and Grace Spotted Eagle, about the sacred practices of this ancient path. These conversations reveal how I was introduced to this ancient medicine way. The chapter entitled <u>Singing a New Memory</u> speaks specifically about the communication that exists beyond the veil of the mundane as a form of telepathy. We also discuss our connection to all life forms. The chapter entitled <u>Wallace Black Elk Speaks</u> illustrates an example of how he lectured about this pathway in a circle. The chapter entitled <u>Seven Sacred Fires</u> reveals how much preparation went into helping people move their consciousness to a higher octave in our Wilderness Gardens teachings. The chapter entitled <u>In Two Worlds I Walk</u> provides an overview of my early footsteps on this sacred path. <u>The Sacred Pipe</u> contains a description of how I was given my own Chanunpa, by Red Buffalo and Black Elk. This writing chronicles how a real human-being walks in service for others. Details of how Black Elk acquired his sacred pipe and a brief history of the Chanunpa-carrier tradition are described. The chapter entitled <u>Looking at the Sun They Dance</u> includes some of my conversations with Red Buffalo at his Sun Dance near the Yankton Reservation in South Dakota. A window of understanding this ancient rite is revealed through several Sun Dances I participated in as a singer at the Sun Dance drum. Regarding the unusual healing that surrounds this path, none was more powerful for me, than when Red Buffalo and I completed a healing ceremony for one of my sons, who was considered legally blind in one eye. Details about that ceremony are revealed in the chapter entitled <u>Healing and Help</u>. This chapter chronicles real moments of doctoring by the nature spirits as well as some of my mentor's explanations about the healing work they helped facilitate as sacred men. Details about one of the most powerful ways a wichasa wakan enhances their spiritual knowledge comes in the chapters entitled <u>Lakota Vision Quest-Hanbleycha</u> and <u>Council with Eagles</u>. These chapters each document this ancient sacred practice as I experienced it. My directions regarding these matters, and teachings for others by Red Buffalo and Black Elk are included.

The chapter entitled <u>Stone Dreamers-Yuwipi Men</u> documents the ancient healing and seeing practices of shamans who are tied up prior to performing this ceremony and then let loose by the spirits at its culmination. The chapter entitled <u>House Ceremony</u> documents a form of healing ceremony that both Black Elk and Red Buffalo facilitated when a stone-people-lodge was not available or a person that needed help was not able to crawl into a lodge. The chapter entitled <u>Medicine Stone</u> documents how I received my first such stone and how it eventually was put to use. Perhaps the most powerful time I spent with Grandfather Black Elk occurred inside the Great Pyramid in Giza, Egypt. A description of this ceremony and what occurred can be found in the chapters entitled <u>Initiation</u> and <u>Ancient Mystery</u>. The chapter entitled <u>Red Hawk</u> documents the naming ceremony in which the spirits gave me my new name with Grandfather Black Elk presiding. <u>Black Elk Teachings-Viejas</u>

Reservation offers an overview of his teaching the year following our Great Pyramid experience. This knowledge is compiled from the many ceremonies and talks we had on that Reservation near my last assignment as a Supervising Park Ranger. Angel Dialogue-San Diego, California is a condensed question and answer meditation that illuminates my continued relationship with my angel after my Great Pyramid Initiation. Bear Butte, South Dakota: Hanbleycha documents what occurred to me on this sacred Lakota vision quest site. Sacred Clowns-Heyoka Wichasas documents a heyoka stone-people-lodge ceremony and brings into focus this misunderstood group of sacred men. Shamanic Equilibrium explains what transpired with me at this threshold of my practice. My family move to Washington State is also documented. Angel Dialogue-Washington State documents a condensed question and answer meditation during this phase of my progression on this pathway. Orca

<u>Nation</u> documents my progression as a neophyte shaman including whales as spiritual allies. It also speaks to my first employment in the northwest on the San Juan Islands. <u>Epilogue</u> answers many questions I am frequently asked about angels and gives the reader a glimpse of my current status.

This writing covers the years of my direct training with my shaman mentors, and a bit more. Grandfather explained that, "We never graduate from this school of knowledge, the more you know, the more there is to know." Because he practiced this life-way over many more years than most North American shamans of our era, I believe he was one of the most knowledgeable ever to have walked with these powers. I traveled with him on three continents to learn all that I could about what I began to refer over time to as the "Sacred Way". During that period of my life my worldly responsibilities were juggled with my spiritual responsibilities until there came a moment when they became one and the same. Therefore, I have not been a casual observer of this pathway as is the case with many who have attempted to write about these ways.

Due to the difficult nature of this material I have modified grammar and condensed sentence structure so as to clarify our discussions. In so doing I have been meticulous about honoring the original intent and context of my talks with my teachers, Wallace Black Elk and Steve Red Buffalo. I have used English phonetic spellings of many Lakota words so you speak and hear the word more like it would sound in that language. In place of medicine man or woman I utilize the Lakota term *wichasa wakan*, "sacred man, or shaman". Because of the humble nature of a Lakota sacred man they are often referred to as *icshe wichasas*, "the humble men".

My mentors were gregarious, loving, courageous, caring, human beings who explored the inner realms of being human, and taught me about navigating the space and time of those worlds . Those shamans that I knew were not sorcerers, sages, or saints. Nor did they ever portray themselves as such. "A sacred man knows he is no better or worse than other men, Grandfather Black Elk explained to me," I am just a man who often walks precariously at the edge of the abyss to accomplish my work serving others". This statement speaks for itself.

Recent failed attempts by untrained individuals to harness these powers should serve as warnings to anyone who thinks these matters are not serious. At no time should anyone attempt these practices without proper training and supervision.

Where a persons' words are easily understood I utilize actual statements by those who take part in the conversations.

The events that transpired remain unaltered.
Time deepens the wonder.

A SACRED WAY

You are about to follow my footsteps onto an ancient sacred pathway that may reveal to you how certain phenomenal occurrences and physical manifestations become possible in ordinary reality. This document may also reveal to you how to bring your own light, wisdom, and compassion into the world. After studying these events for the last twenty-five years it is my belief that a shaman is sometimes able to merge non-ordinary reality with ordinary reality to help facilitate healing, curing, seeing, or being. Often we utilize the help of our spiritual allies.

My primary teachers were called wichasa wakans. These men or women are a very small circle within the larger circle of Lakota that are known as the Sioux nation. They were called the "Earth People" and the "Peace People" by their ancient contemporaries. They were located in the center of Turtle Island on the great plains of North America.

At the real center of these people was the path of the sun, moon, planets, and stars. They considered this their sacred way. They held a reverence for the passing of the four seasons within their sacred way. They also realized that all natural things in the universe had their own sacred way of sharing a balance with each other. The sacred way, our reality, is not one point in space moving in only one direction. The sacred way, which includes our lives, they knew to be a circle without end. The elders divulge that during a past age we humans understood that we were a part of the whole. We understood that we were no greater or lesser then the rest of the beings on the circle of life, just of a different consciousness, and we lived our lives with respect for all things. We had awareness about the energetic light that connects each of us that they referred to as Great Spirit. It is said that in our world, over the mists of time, human beings lost their harmony with the rest of the beings on the circle of life… and many of our capabilities were forgotten. It is essential to honor all things on the circle of life. I know that all beings share a part of the consciousness of the primary creative force and that each being acts as a mirror to form our world.

We are each potential holders of the central flame -pure divinity. Having discovered this sublime reality, I am sometimes filled with knowledge and great power. It is then that I walk hand in hand with nature and mirror the strength of the

Great Mother, lit by that instinct which contains wisdom. In that inner sanctuary I am sometimes able to find the subtle essence of the soul of Nature herself.

Come sit with me as you read this document and share the Chanunpa of understanding and interface with the intangible field of energies I call spirits. Learn how a wichasa wakan is able to walk between worlds. If you continue reading, it may be possible for you to establish your own relationship with this Sacred Way.

DEDICATION

For my parents James and Lily who brought me into this world and nurtured me "in the light". Those words are the Dutch translation of our last name. Their generosity and giving to others was a remarkable example for me to follow.

For my lovely wife Carol, my three sons, their wives, and my grandchildren, who taught me that love is the beginning of all wisdom. Carol was also instrumental in laying this book out prior to publishing.

For my sisters Karen and Gaylen who have encouraged me on many occasions. Karen also offered valuable advice about how my story could be told in the early stages of this manuscript taking shape.

For Linda who learned many of the ancient songs to help me perform the ceremonies to help others and was always willing to do whatever task put before her to bring about a successful outcome.

For Catherine whose attention to detail in the final stages of completion of this manuscript was very helpful.

For those who have attained access to the multi-dimensional realms of nature and humbly serve humanity in relative obscurity.

For Wallace Black Elk and Steve Red Buffalo, who gave so much of themselves to help so many people and extended a magic thread of their lineage to me. I honor their biological families and the sacrifices that they made to allow their fathers to follow the voices of Spirit.

For all of you who have found your own sacred way, I urge you to enter this pure awareness with courage, endurance, alertness, and love. Black Elk's words echo in my mind.

O mitakuye oyasin, "To all my relations".

CHAPTER 1
BEGINNINGS

The blazing sun had started on its descent to the distant horizon. A steady light breeze was blowing that late afternoon. It was a usual occurrence in that part of northern San Diego County, California, west of Palomar mountain observatory. The breeze was a gift from the not too distant Pacific Ocean. The canyon walls along the San Luis Rey River on the western rim of Pauma Valley were changing color like a chameleon sitting on a rosy toned peach. The former owner of the 584 acres I now lived and worked on, Manchester

Body, would have loved to have developed a camellia of that exotic color. Beginning in the mid 1950's and for the next fifteen years he had planted rooted cuttings among the magnificent stands of native trees creating a medieval tapestry of camellia bushes of pink, saucy red, opulent white, and blushing rose blossoms. He had added plants such as shiny leafed holly, variegated pittosporum, pampas grass, fremontia, bottle brush, eucalyptus, oleanders, and many others, to create a menagerie of colors and textures before he died. After first seeing the property, I worked through the appropriate channels within my parks bureaucracy to look into turning the grounds into a park that could be utilized by the public. After producing a conceptual document for the administration, I was given that opportunity.

It was the heart of summer when most of the wild flowers had long since bloomed and then vanished. The faces of lupine, chocolate lilies, brodea,

Chinese houses, shooting stars, windmill pinks, and all the rainbowed others would remain hidden until next spring-vanishing memories stored away by the passing of the seasons.

The sky was still a visible cerulean blue. A multi-rayed sunset of orange peels and daffodil petals was on its way to be followed by a light show from the Milky Way that appeared to reveal an ancient treasure map of light across a Van Gogh like starry night.

The glory of the setting sun had fixed my attention on the shadows of the massive gnarled and gargoyle like ancient coast live oak trees encircling my home. As I gazed at them I detected new shades of burnt umber, golden honey, and a multitude of gray and brown earth tones, oozing from their grooved and pitted surfaces.

My mind shifted to the anthropologist that had introduced himself to me several weeks before. Dr. William Lyon stated that he represented

Wallace Black Elk and Grace Spotted Eagle. He added that he was recommending our Preserve as a possible place for his well-known associate and wife to do some teaching in. He emphasized that Wallace Black Elk and his *half-side* "wife", would make that decision after discussing details with me on a visit planned sometime over the next month. That visit had been scheduled for this day. They were approaching on the mile and a half trail to my stone cottage. During that time of the evening I could hear the *poor-jill-ip* cry of a Poor-will in the distance. Flushed, they flutter up like a gray brown moth in the arid hills along the wild trails to our house. I knew someone was coming.

I had worked most of that day on my parks' barn restoration project. The weathered structure had fallen into disrepair after a fire had gutted it a decade before my parks' department had taken over the property. Manchester Body had run the Los Angeles Daily News for years, and began publishing <u>Leaves From An Editors Notebook</u> from the barn during his years on the grounds. His purpose was to "share with our family of readers the calmness of the everlasting hills, the soothing music of the singing streams, the beauty of the 100,000 camellias and azaleas growing beneath a virgin forest of oaks and many acres of wild flowers." He had published his newsletter out of what now had the appearance of a partially burnt Noah's Ark with its charred spans still exposed to the elements in a diminished two-story rectangle. Tin roof pieces had been removed and stacked for future replacement. It was located approximately fifty yards into the old oak forest from the entrance to our home. As I sat on my front porch I wondered how they had put out the fire without the entire valley going up in smoke. Park volunteers and I had acquired matching pieces of barn wood from dilapidated relics throughout the region to restore the structure as a future interpretive center. My thoughts drifted to my uncle Christian Nielsen who had been apprenticed at the young age of eight years as a carpenter in Denmark. He had built the plaster and brick single story rambler house I grew up in for my mother and father in the Central Valley of California, and had become a respected home builder in that area.

Making Wilderness Gardens into an oasis of peace and tranquility to educate people became a labor of love for me in those days. A sanctuary where man could co-exist with the wildlife- including 140 different species of birds, made it a special piece of earth on the outskirts of San Diego civilization. Now a casino can be seen on the edge of the property. Much of the oak forest has died off. Most of the glorious camellias my staff and I used to water by hand have vanished. The wildlife populations have been decimated including the river itself due to the ground table lowering from nearby development and agriculture. But back then we lived with squirrels, rabbits, coyotes, bobcats, opossums, raccoons, deer, mountain lions, reptiles, and so many others. Damselflies, dragon flies, and butterflies threaded their way along the ponds where bass and blue gill flourished. I was the only paid staff member at the facility, which meant I utilized the "Friends" group of docents that supported the park, civilian volunteers, probation personnel, California Conservation Corp., and an occasional Park Ranger on loan from another facility to manage and maintain that unique acreage. Bordering the preserve were the La Jolla, Pauma, Mesa Grande, Rincon, and Santa Isabel Indian reservations to the East, and the Mission and Pala reservations to the North and West.

On the day we met Wallace Black Elk and his wife Grace Spotted Eagle had strolled from their vehicle parked beyond the footbridge at the park entrance beneath the crest of the chaparral laden ridge line, a mile and a half away. They had entered the trail to our house at the river. Dr. Lyon had informed him that our meeting was to take place at the Ranger's house. As they strolled past our elfin forest of buckwheat, ceanothus, sugar bush, scrub oak, manzanita, and wild elderberry, he had spotted many specimens of white sage and black sage, which he had used medicinally and in ceremony on his trips through California. When they entered the oak forest they could hear frogs singing by our river. The sound had brought back memories of the rattles he had been taught to tune to their songs by his grandparents when he was a boy back in South Dakota.

As he knocked on the screen door to our home they heard my children playing inside. I remember hearing Spotted Eagle comment to Black Elk about the stiffened joints in her legs as she stepped back off the concrete steps to the earthen path at the entrance to our stone and brick cottage. Before me stood a Native American of considerable size. He looked to be several inches over six feet tall. He had sturdy round faced coffee toned features. Though an elder his broad shoulders and muscular frame indicated to me he was still physically fit. He wore a wide brimmed straw hat with a colorfully beaded headband. His silver graying black braids extended to his shoulders over a plaid long sleeved light cotton cowboy shirt. Hanging loosely around his neck was a silver eagle necklace. A large silver belt buckled his blue jeans. His tennis shoes remained untied, serving as modern day moccasins.

Standing by his side was a petite regal looking woman barely covering five-feet. She possessed piercing dark eyes set into a more oval shaped face framed by graying black hair tied behind her head. She wore a cotton blue flower patterned dress, and dark colored walking shoes like my own Montana born grandmother used to wear.

His head was bowed forward as he stood upon our wagon wheel framed doorstep. His wife was partially hidden behind his large sturdy torso. I could not see his eyes during that initial moment due to the tilt to his head-and yet I felt his strength. When he finally looked at me I could see the kindness within those dark luminescent spheres. He then smiled and extended his hand.

"O mi tak u ye oyasin," he said. "My name is Wallace Black Elk. This is my half-side Grace Spotted Eagle."

I noted his grip was powerful and his hands were callused like mine.

I responded, "Hello, my name is Torrey."

I would learn later those initial words in his native tongue were the keys to unlocking the secrets of this man.

"What can I do for you two?" I cordially stated.

"We would like to talk to you about doing some teaching here," He stated the words firmly.

"Would you like a cup of coffee?" I responded in a matter of fact tone.

"We could go into my house and talk about what you have in mind. Does that suit you?"

"*Washte*, Good," was his simple reply. No words had come forth from the serene but obviously strong woman by his side. Nevertheless, I felt she was somehow peering inside my soul while I talked. They followed me down our white-bricked hallway into the kitchen with its' matching white cupboards and beige with brown speckled linoleum flooring. We sat at our circular well-used oak table in the dining nook, which faced out to several five hundred year old towering coast live oaks that were posed around those grounds like a dancing tribe of druids. The sage scrub understory and various granite outcroppings added to the rugged beauty of the area. Usually a rattlesnake or two could be found not far away.

I remember comparing this couple to local Native Americans from our community. He was much taller and more muscular than any of my friends. The reverse was true for his wife who seemed smaller and more petite than most of the native women of our region. As they sat back in their chairs I could see they were now studying my wife Carol and I. I had grown lean and muscular from all the physical labor at the park and wore my sandy- blond hair modestly long over the collar of my shirt which filled out the broad shoulders I had inherited from my own hard working athletic father. I thought Black Elk was taller than me by a couple of inches. In those years I maintained a bushy mustache and my usually sun-burned Scandinavian complexion gifted me a red tone year round. My blue-green eyes twinkled back at them. My wife Carol in those years wore her naturally curly reddish brown hair down to her shoulders framing her slender features and smooth fair complexion. The green eyed mother of our three children radiated an inner beauty and confidence that matched her outer beauty during our exchange.

I poured our coffee and settled into the chair across from them. Carol listened from the cutting board a few yards away intent on finishing the cookies she had started before their arrival. My three sons had moved to the pond for some evening fishing time with our two golden retriever dogs and park volunteer who helped with the boys on many occasions.

"You are the one," he said, sounding quite surprised.

"If you mean by your statement-am I in charge? Yes, I am responsible for this park," I responded.

"No-No-No-you are the one that the spirits told me we were to teach," he said. Startled, I leaned forward a minute because the fading light was doing something unusual to his face-he seemed a bit fuzzy.

In that instant, I flashed back to my plea-about a month earlier. It was for a wise teacher to help me unravel some of the occurrences of the deepest connections to the natural world that I had been experiencing. My years of living in the peace and solitude of that natural space had heightened my awareness in unusual ways. A recent example was the vision of the face of a woman that had appeared to me just prior to my release of a great horned owl back into the wilds. I had been a volunteer for Wildlife Rehab for several years and had successfully saved many area raptors from the ravages of a culture intent on putting poisons in its orchards. This action killed off the very predator that would have kept in balance pests they were trying to do away with. An Indian woman's face had appeared in place of that owls' face. It did not disappear until the release had taken place. On my night walks through that wilderness I had also become aware of the little flashes of light that seemed to be transmitted in some cosmic form of Morse code throughout the forest. I was actually seeing how the forest was interconnected by energies only seen by a few others. I had also begun to sense the subtle powers of the stones. They drew me to them placed along the river's edge by many years of water and earth movements. Many of those stones were magnificent and seemed to be able to give something vital to the people who could tune in. A subtle universe was beginning to open up to me.

I wondered then if the man before me was nature's response to my prayer on the turtle-like rock meditation site at our rivers edge. That particular stone reminded me of a giant version of the turtles I used to buy at the pet stores in California where I was raised.

I found it curious to have this remembrance and the thought brought me back into focus.

"We have been called here," he emphasized each word.

"Spirit has sent us here to teach you about our way of viewing the universe, the earth mother, the creator, and the Chanunpa." He smiled calmly at me.

For a moment he seemed like someone from another planet. I believed what he said about them being sent here, but I did not then understand any of it.

"We are the Lakota, the Earth People, the Peace People. Your books call us Sioux. That was never our real name. We all have a biological father and mother but our real father is Creator and our real mother is the Earth." I remember his voice was smooth and mellow sounding.

"*Mitakuye oyasin* means, " to all my relations". It helps to be reminded that we are related to everything that exists. We are part of the fire, and the rock, and the water, and the plants. Each has a spirit. Each has a consciousness. You are familiar with that connection, but many human beings have forgotten."

The elder shaman frowned. He looked at me to verify that I understood. He seemed to already know that I had made some unusual connections to my environment.

He arched his eyebrows, "I have trained many years, in this way. I began when I was a little boy and I am an old man now," he said with authority and then broke out into a huge grin. His dark friendly eyes then pierced me with grave intent.

"The life on this pathway is not an easy life," he said as if remembering some of those hardships that very moment might serve as a warning to me. He paused for several seconds as if he were waking from a dream and then continued. He asked us if we would like to hear a story of his. Carol sat down next to me as he began after our positive response. We had become silent before he began with a theatrical movement of his hand as if he was clearing the room of any negative energy.

"Many years ago when I was a young man, I was way up on a hill praying for a vision. We call that *hanbleycha*. I was having a hard time. I was having a really hard time…no food…no water…one of my hardest stretches…then after several days…our entire solar system was revealed to me. Right before my own eyes… I could see stars around me… and a Spirit showed me the powers of the universe. There was the Creator with his wisdom. Below was the knowledge of our Mother the Earth. I saw a man standing in the middle of all this. I saw fire. There was water. An eagle was standing on this altar. Each time it lifted its wing I saw a fire underneath it. Then it flapped its wing and a tremendous wind spiraled clockwise. At the center of the spiral was the sun, and on its edge was this rock-the earth. There were planets going around it."

Then Spirit said, "When you return to earth tell your people to love each other and walk behind the sacred pipe."

"I realized then that Great Spirit had given me a power and it was not to be taken lightly. They blessed me through the Chanunpa."

Black Elk continued, "*Cha* means "wood". The stem of the pipe is made of wood. *Nunpa* means "two". It is our *tree of life.* The base of a Chanunpa is made of a sacred stone your people call catlinite. It is found in a thinly bedded layer about 12 to 18 inches thick. It is sandwiched between massive layers of a much harder stone called quartzite. Scientists say the pipestone was a clay material and the quartzite was a sand deposited at the bottom of the sea about one billion years ago. As these beds began to move over time and uplift some of the pipestone began to be seen at what is now a park in Pipestone, Minnesota. The Grandfathers and Grandmothers say that Creator made our pipestone from the blood of the people of a past age. We connect those male and female pieces together and use that sacred pipe to communicate with Great Spirit. Over my years of training I have been given a power over the four winds, 'over space and time', with that sacred implement."

I felt an odd feeling in the pit of my stomach. "You are the one I was told about by the spirits to teach." He stated it again, and now this mysterious elder had my complete attention.

"Grandfather Creator and Grandmother Earth bring help through the sacred pipe. The amount of help depends on the circumstances and our intentions," he replied. He talked on about his Chanunpa. "I grew up with the knowledge of the power of the sacred pipe. When we approach the spiritual realm in the correct manner-with appropriate intent and gratitude, we are able to acquire help from the greatest powers of our universe"

My mind moved back to the time in Montana that I had utilized such a device with a group of Flathead Indian elders. That sweat- lodge ceremony had left a lasting impression on me. Even the scent of the pine boughs we sat on was still fresh in my memory. I wondered if I would have been so open to what Black Elk was proposing for the teaching at the Preserve if I had not had such a favorable opinion of that sacred ritual. I was 21 then. I thought of it as a true philosopher's stone. I briefly explained how my cousin and I, while looking for a place to camp on a Montana adventure, had driven to the edge of a clearing of log cabins burning and native elders sitting on the earth in a daze after losing their homes. We had offered them the fish we had caught the day before as dinner that night. As serendipity played out we stayed several days to help them and were asked to take part in a sweat-lodge ceremony before we left. Black Elk was now informing me that the correct translation for sweat-lodge was stone-people-lodge.

"You were blessed to have that experience within that sacred space.

It is where we go to purify ourselves and to make many deep connections to spirit. That upside down basket of woven willow saplings, tied together with twine and covered with blankets or hides to hold in the heat, is a place where a person is able to increase their understanding of our universe. You must stay aware. When we bring the stones inside they are treated as another part of the intelligence of our planet. We put a prayer in each stone that we bring into our ceremonies. We heat them in a sacred way with the help from one of our great gifts from spirit-which is fire. When we pour water over the stones to produce a steam, we call that 'the breath of life'. There are many medicines on this pathway."

His words reminded me of the ancient alchemists who were said to be able to turn lead into gold and do many other amazing feats of healing. I wondered if there could be a connection to those alchemists through earth, air, fire, water, and Spirit.

I then shared the legend passed along to me by the local population, that our valley had served as an ancient Luiseno tribal healing ground and went on to explain my own direction on those grounds. "The news of environmental traumas assails us on every side. Unseasonal storms, floods, fires, drought, melting ice caps, lost species of flora and fauna, rising sea levels, and disappearing ozone layer leave us on the brink of the abyss. Our teaching here is centered on helping people be more connected to this beautiful natural space, and therefore the entire planet. I believe one of my primary mandates here has been to enlighten people about the importance of our relationship to the earth. I believe we must build more efficient shelters, grow more vibrant foods, simplify our needs, pool our resources, and evolve more responsive communities. We must help people understand the importance of nurturing more loving relationships to the earth and each other. In many ways our present course is a reality gone mad. When we stop our war against the earth we will stop our wars against each other. I would be honored to bring the teaching you each have to share here."

Black Elk said they were looking forward to sharing their philosophy and sacred ways in the near future. He broke into a wide grin. Then just as suddenly a sad expression replaced the happy peaceful look on his face.

"Those children that you teach in your outdoor classes are very fortunate," he said with a nod. "When I was a young boy the government took many of us away from our homes and forced us into their schools. They cut our hair and changed our clothes to uniforms. They forced us to speak English. If we spoke our own language they would wash our mouths out with laundry detergent. If we didn't say a word right they would clip a clothespin to our ears. They would make us hold out our palms and they would hit our hands. Sometimes we would bleed. There were times when the ruler would break. Other times I would not understand a lesson and they would make me stand on my tiptoes until finally I could not stand any more. Then they would beat me."

"I did not want to go to school so I would hide out with my Grandma and Grandpa. When we prayed with our Chanunpas and conducted our ceremonies to talk with the Great Mystery, the government would then come onto our land and break everything. We spent time in their jails because we honored Great Spirit and were attempting to live the harmony of this path… they refused to understand."

Black Elk glanced at his wife with an expression that said that he was through talking for that evening. She exchanged pleasantries with Carol before they left.

We exchanged phone numbers and he said he and Dr. William Lyon would be in touch with me to go over plans for a special teaching we could accomplish together at the park and then they disappeared down our trail through our forest of oaks back to the park entrance. I had no idea then how that meeting would change my life.

CHAPTER 2
SACRED MEN AND WOMEN- WICHASA WAKANS

Communication with nature spirits, healing, curing, seeing, dimensional travel, and even weather changes, over the course of my apprenticeship, became a part of my conversations with my mentors. "By our thinking and intention we are able to help facilitate ordinary and extraordinary reality. Some people call this shifting of our focus a trance," Black Elk stated.

Shamans throughout the world are known to have a special relationship with fire, heat, and light. Shaman is derived from the Vedic term *sram*, meaning "to heat oneself". A *shaman* is considered "a master of fire and the embodiment of a heat so fierce that its spiritual luminescence is associated with both purity and knowledge". The oriental word *shuman* means "the essence of the most important thing for entering the Truth-as through a gate". The Lakota wichasa wakan certainly can be found within each of these definitions.

According to Grandfather Nicholas Black Elk as told by Wallace, because of what a wichasa wakan provided a tribe in the way of body, mind, or spiritual assistance, their food and shelter were always taken care of by those he assisted. "A Chanunpa-carrier could walk from one side of *Turtle Island* , "North America" to the other and never have to worry about his basic requirements for survival. Because of the changes in how we provide for ourselves in our modern world a sacred man or woman's living expenses become a serious drawback to our survival in this day and age. In spite of carrying out our work to perfection there is sometimes no money or resources to help the wichasa wakan function in his sacred role. Whenever possible, ceremonial supplies are provided by those requesting help. However, because of the poverty on many reservations, life is sometimes very hard for those of us still doing this work."

In our early conversations by telephone, Black Elk related he had been practicing his unique form of the sacred way longer than most North American indigenous elders. He had practiced for sixty years at that time. He explained how he had begun his sacred education with eleven Grandfathers and Grandmothers at an unprecedented early age of five years. He considered Grandfather Nicholas Black Elk to have played a major role in keeping the ways of the wichasa wakan alive for future generations and realized how important his teaching had been to him.

My initial impression of Wallace Black Elk was that he was a brilliant man able to discuss many topics of interest very fluently. He explained that he still had to think in Lakota and speak in English. He usually felt deficient in English. However, I found that not to be so. I became aware over time that he hid behind the-I-do-not-understand image, to see who he was dealing with. Then in the same way a deer peers out from the forest to make sure everything is all right for his next movements, the forest branches parted and Grandfather revealed himself. This attitude would be considered one use of *deer medicine,* when a gift from a specific animal nation is utilized.

Grandfather was able to hold a conversation with a physicist just as easily as a park ranger naturalist. We talked about the uses of plants to help people on our walks in my park. He also enjoyed listening for bird songs along our trails and watching for any four legged tracks left behind in the soil. Because of my naturalist skills in ethnobotany, ornithology, and herpetology, I believe there were times he tried to help me understand the old ways from a scientific viewpoint. Some of our initial conversations were about the physics of what a wichasa wakan or icshe wichasa was able to accomplish with the help of Great Spirit. We discussed a recent stone-people-lodge he had performed where a group of scientists had experienced many of the visible phenomena of his ceremonies such as lights in the air, shapes of animals moving about, or little lightnings dancing within the confines of a deep space created within. He related one such physicist's view that energy with frequencies faster than the speed of light comprise, a world of super physical reality. The physicist felt that when those super energies decelerate, substance and form materialize. Thereby, explaining from a scientific viewpoint some of the unusual happenings within his ceremonies. "Grandson,

Tunkashila is the greatest scientist. No man can duplicate his creation. Look at a tree, an ant, a bird, a four legged, the sky, a star. No man can duplicate them." He wanted me to realize that the circles of science and native wisdom were converging. Yet he always came back to the fact that Great Spirit was responsible for anything that was accomplished. It was of prime importance that a sacred man not ever take credit for a positive result. He also felt that certain aspects of what he helped accomplish would simply remain a part of the Great Mystery.

During a subsequent telephone conversation, Black Elk explained that another wichasa wakan would be coming to help me prepare for the encampment, lecture, and sacred rituals. At the time I thought he meant that individual would be coming to help with the physical preparation for the event.

Several weeks later I got my first glance of him. Steve Red Buffalo, an adopted son of Black Elks, appeared younger than Black Elk by a dozen years or so. Red Buffalo had collar length straight black hair that framed his smiling rugged coffee toned features. He found my sons and my wife and I involved in playing a baseball game underneath the oaks at the entrance to our house on that warm summer evening.

As he stepped toward us in Levi blue jeans, black cowboy boots, and a red plaid cowboy shirt, I realized he was about my height. His black felt cowboy hat was accented with a simple leather headband. It was tilted back as if to release some of his exhaustion from their trip. When I peered into his intense dark eyes they expressed warmth, kindness, and a distant sadness. His broad shoulders were reminiscent of his revered Lakota namesake-the Buffalo. He looked strong enough to wrestle one.

"O mi ta kuye oyasin, Torrey. Nice to meet you. Wallace told me you were expecting us." He had introduced himself with quiet confidence.

"I would like you to meet Bill. He came to help us with the teaching this weekend. Bill has been helping Wallace and Grace as a ceremonial singer in their teaching activities. His mom is Black Elk's sister."

They had arrived in Black Elk's pick-up truck. Red Buffalo had travelled to Denver from the Yankton Reservation in eastern South Dakota to meet Bill. They had driven straight through from Denver to San Diego. The truck was packed to overflowing with tipi and ceremonial supplies, drums, medicine bundles, buckets, ladles, a propane cook- stove, sleeping bags, and other miscellaneous gear all tied off under a huge tarp. They confirmed Black Elk and Spotted Eagle were expected to arrive later in the week.

"This is beautiful out here," Bill said to no one in particular. He looked thin and wiry in his tank top that read "Indian Power". He wore blue jeans, tennis shoes, and his long shoulder length black hair hung straight to his shoulders. His dark eyes revealed a melancholy and a wondering about who I might be as a bureaucrat in charge of that natural area.

I tried to put them at ease over dinner. The soup and sandwiches helped create an instant bond between my family and these two men. My three sons and wife took an instant liking to both of them. This was always an important signal to me regarding who someone really was on the inside. They had many questions about Wilderness Gardens which I answered patiently. Red Buffalo wanted to know how long we had lived there and did they really pay me for that opportunity? I explained I had started coming to the area from my previous park assignment to help with small projects prior to our family coming to live here in January 1981, after my proposal for the area had been accepted by my department.

I related to them how in my beginnings there I chose not to take my wife and the boys to see our new house until I had cleared out all the wildlife that had moved in over its unoccupied years. The mice, wood rats, squirrels, tarantulas, and scorpions were never welcome again inside. After several weeks of cleaning and a little paint and tender loving care I received Carol's kiss of approval. We moved in soon afterwards with the help of family and many friends.

My new South Dakota friends asked about the rattlesnake population and I informed them that the grounds were quite abundant with western pacific, red-diamond, and sidewinder varieties. Not knowing their feelings about snakes I explained they simply needed to stay aware. I went on to inform them that it was too hot that time of year for much activity from them. I did relate a bit of my own history with the snake population, revealing that a five and a half foot red-diamond rattler had bitten and killed one of my golden retrievers, Hawn, several years before. Our veterinarian fought all night to save our dog but he eventually lost that battle. I explained they needed to be careful but that the snakes usually minded their own business. I had even stepped on a few without problems. I explained that I had pointed out to many of my park patrons that the triangular head of a snake meant they were poisonous, and we had a healthy population of several non-poisonous varieties as well. Bill then replied, "Speaking of poisonous, what about all the poison oak"? I let them know that the poison oak was quite evident under the oaks and that 'leaflets three-let them be',was good advice. I was one of the fortunate few who could actually hold the plant with no adverse reaction. "Some people are not allergic to its oils", I added. I went on to explain to them that the bass and blue gill were abundant in the larger of our two lakes and also let them know they could utilize our family raft if they wanted to pole around and enjoy the views. I later showed them where I stored our fishing gear if time permitted.

The next day, after I had completed a small project at the barn, Red Buffalo asked if I might want to learn how to set up a tipi with Bill. I had never set up a tipi before, and I told him I would love that opportunity. He informed me it would allow him a chance to scout the river for stones and willow for our teaching and ceremonies.

Before he began his hike I received a taste of his direct teaching style:

"An 18 foot tipi doesn't get assembled with the speed and ease of your modern day tents," he said with a grin. First you will need to clear the brush and pebbles off the ground of a circle similar to the tipi's diameter. Tipi coverings are now made of canvas instead of the buffalo hides sewn together from the good old days. You will need to spread out your covering in an open area. Three lodge poles can then be selected and placed to form a tripod which you will rope off at their gathering point. The other lodge poles, all taller than the height of the canvass by several feet are placed around your original tripod evenly to hold the canvas skin of the structure in a pyramidal upright fashion. Two poles are utilized to hoist the canvas in place over the other poles. These are then ready to adjust for proper fit, position, and tension. Rope them off at the point where they all intersect appropriately. The two poles you utilized to lift your canvas in place are your wind flap positioning devices. These act as your adjusters for the winds outside that might affect your camp fire inside. They are to be moved if the wind direction changes. The inner liner is attached to the inner walls of the tipi at each pole. This creates a drafting effect up and out the smoke hole at the peak of the structure. Have fun."

"I will check in on your progress after I locate what we will need for our sacred teaching," he directed as he disappeared into the thickets of willow and alder.

The sound of branches cracking behind us sounded like wet wood on an open campfire. It caused me to turn in time to see Red Buffalo walking up a mule deer path to where Bill and I were standing. The tipi erecting process had taken us several hours.

"The spirits here tell me we need to build our tipi in the meadow that the stone-people-lodges will be in. I hope you guys aren't too upset with me over the change. I will catch up to you over there." He then continued on his hike along the stream. He had appeared and vanished behind a dense patch of buckwheat, ceanothus, and a gnarled coast live oak tree upon which hung wild grape vines like garlands on a Christmas tree.

Bill and I looked at each other and smiled sheepishly, knowing how much effort we had put forth to assemble everything in the vicinity of the river. We began the take down process while laughing at each other and began our rebuilding project by the second lake where Red Buffalo had redirected us. This time we were a little more efficient in our movements together. We decreased our time of assembly to almost half of our first attempt.

Just as we had put the last wind flap pole in place Red Buffalo appeared again out of the woods behind us with a peculiar look on his face.

"Ho, men, I have some new information from my spiritual guides. The tipi needs to be relocated by the lake closest to your house Torrey, across from this meadow. They say we will now need to utilize that area instead of where you're working because of the larger crowd that is expected. Another tipi will arrive for the teaching so we can split the changing area for men and women there." Bill and I were silent.

"The tipi is sacred architecture," he stated emphatically in my direction as if to change the touchy subject of relocation. "The shape of the tipi coverings in the form that they wrap around the poles, can be found if you slice across the bark near the top of a cottonwood tree," he stated with a twinkle in his eye.

Neither Bill nor I expressed any outward sign of anger with the spirit's new plan. After asking exactly where the tipi needed to be placed and walking over there together and back, we again dismantled our work of art and assembled it by the appropriate lake. We had cut our assembly time in half once again.

In the process Bill and I had become friends and had refined our expertise in tipi assembly. He called us *kolas*, "friends", in his Lakota language. While we worked together he shared stories about his life. "My people moved westward out of Minnesota where they abandoned the woodlands for the freedom of the plains. We hunted the buffalo and acquired our horse skills there. It was abundant with deer and birds, and many wild edible plants and plenty of fresh water. The Black Hills overlooked those hunting grounds. The slopes and peaks were so heavily wooded with dark pines they actually looked black to our ancestors. The first white settlers came around 1800 and you know the rest of that sad tale. I live in Denver but I get out to the "Rez" when I can. The sense of the sacred seems to be missing nowadays in how people interact with the Earth Mother. There seems to be a selfishness and ambition in that relationship rather than the love and respect that the old ones had for all that was natural."

He also explained that his Uncle Wallace had been one of the spiritual leaders at the Wounded Knee II confrontation between the government and the Lakota people in 1973. For seventy-one days a few hundred men, women, and children had challenged a large paramilitary force by staging a demonstration to bring to the world's attention how our government had mistreated its native populations through a trail of broken treaties and horrible conditions on many reservations. It was even more significant that they had made their stand at the site where one of the greatest tragedies ever to take place on American soil had occurred. It was on those grounds that our government had slaughtered hundreds of unarmed men, women, and children, less than a century before in 1890, in what became known as Wounded Knee I.

Bill became an easy person to talk to regarding what I was going through over the next several years of my training with Red Buffalo and his Uncle Wallace.

CHAPTER 3
PURIFICATION

The next morning the three of us hiked through the oak woodland and retraced some of Red Buffalos steps by the river. We walked under California sycamore and thickets of elder, willow, wild grape, morning glory, datura, poison oak, and our tangle of wild camellias.

Red Buffalo focused his teaching with me on the basics of stone-people-lodge construction that day. In so doing he addressed many beginning aspects of what I would eventually call "the Sacred Way".

"Every step we take in the stone-people-lodge ceremony is a prayer-including the preparations. Today we will ask Great Spirit for permission to take a few willow cuttings for the making of the lodge structure. Each one we harvest, we say a little prayer over, and we leave a little pinch of tobacco for the spirit of that plant. When we do this we say thank you. The willow- nation is abundant here so we will work our way along this section of stream south. Look for pliable sticks about 12-16 feet high, one to two inches thick- like this one. We each should harvest around twenty pieces. If we need more we can acquire those later."

He rested on a large granite boulder as we moved out of sight of each other along the river's edge.

The wrens, flycatchers, flickers, towhees, woodpeckers, and sparrows created a background symphony during the harvest. Cutting the willow with small handsaws was the easy part of the process. Getting them out of the wild thickets over the stream and back to the trail was the major challenge. Several hours later we each emerged with what we needed.

As we loaded them into my truck, Red Buffalo again began to speak, "My people have come to their stone-people-lodges for many generations." He continued in a tone that demanded my attention. "So we crawl inside our lodges to complete an *inipi ceremony* to be "purified". When we pray, whatever our intentions are, the spirits will add power to it. Good words and good thoughts are rewarded by Great Spirit. This must be accomplished with the proper intent focused from your heart and your mind."

"The English description sweat-lodge is just a nickname. When we crawl into the lodge, and the hot stones come in, and we pour water over those stones, naturally we sweat. The spirits have told me the words "sweat- lodge" is not theirs. They call it *tunkan tipi*. "*Tun*" means birth, "*kan*" means age. So the stone-people return to the womb of the Earth Mother in this ceremony and so do we. We put fire back into those stones to make them hot and we also remember the fire that is in each of us. We follow the word "stone" with "people" because they are also beings on the Earth Mother. We say tree-people, plant-people, bird-people, and so on. You have an understanding now".

"When we crawl through that little opening to get into the lodge, we have to crawl on our hands and knees. A person needs to be humble to access this ancient pathway. Then we have our visit with the old ones, those spirits and the ancient and wise stone-people. When we close that door to the lodge, and all the blankets and coverings are in place, the temperature rises, and we exist in the womb of our mother the earth. Time ceases to function in its usual manner. We make prayer offerings and tell our problems, and we use that oxygen and hydrogen together to expel those poisons out of our bodies. We open and close the blankets that serve as a door four times to the light. Each opening is part of the rebirthing process."

As we moved between the alders and willows at the edge of the river he continued this teaching. "The best stones for this ceremony are dense brown volcanic stones about as big as a person's head. These are always our first choice for use in the lodge. For the approaching ceremonies I have scouted and found stones that are not volcanic stones but they will serve us well enough." He showed me what we needed to collect as well as what would not be appropriate. He explained any granite or shale like stones would flake or explode and not hold the heat. Again he asked for a smooth dense stone usually gray in this environment.

We waded along the edge of the banks of the San Luis Rey River until we had selected over seventy stones. The current moved very slowly that time of year. Those stones were added to those that would be brought in for the ceremonies. After carrying them to the park's access road we picked them up with my truck and brought them to our intended lodge site next to the larger of our two lakes. While we worked they began to teach me several of the old ceremonial songs that were utilized in the stone-people-lodge ceremonies. As the sweat poured down my brow from our labors I could not help the smile that creased my mouth.

CHAPTER 4
ANCIENT TRADITIONS

Red Buffalo and Bill had slept soundly in the teepee we set up the day before. A small camp fire inside the structure was heating their coffee when I arrived. They demonstrated how the inner liner helped form a drafting effect to move the smoke up and out the wind flaps at the apex of the inner pyramid-like shape. I invited them to breakfast with my family after our coffee in their now familiar structure. We chuckled around the breakfast table when Bill mentioned that he had seen a picture of me in my John Muir garb-beard, top hat, and period suit prior to arriving. Someone had apparently shown him a newspaper article published on my teaching program at the preserve. He admitted he had expected an older person from the likes of that photo. I explained that I had used the life of John Muir as an interpretive tool to share some of his philosophy with our park patrons. One of my favorite quotes from him, "In wildness is the preservation of the world," was prominently displayed in my entrance kiosk to the grounds. Respect for the beauty and power of the natural world were at the heart of John Muir's writings. That conversation led to our discussion on the influx of Europeans to North America and its effects on indigenous populations.

"In the United States of America, wherever the European settlers went, native peoples died of new diseases. Native populations have been estimated in the millions when the major onslaught began in the 1600's. There are now fewer than one million first people left," Red Buffalo sadly stated. I remained silent.

Bill added, "Several courageous Lakota families never stopped our sacred practices during this devastating and lengthy period of time. For this reason several anthropologists believe that Lakota shamanism is one of the purest, least affected form of shamanism from prehistory. We carried on our ancient ceremonies that connected us to the earth we revered as our true Mother and to the Creator that we knew to be our true Father in spite of the threats that came from the government and religious institutions. The Manifest Destiny Policy of the U.S Government, carried out during the last years of this era, gobbled up our sacred land and limited our freedoms."

I felt as though my new friends were providing me a clear and unobstructed view of how they perceived our world. I had read "Bury My Heart at Wounded Knee" several years before meeting

Bill and Red Buffalo. It had profoundly touched my heart then, and being with those two kind and generous souls made me embarrassed for our government and what had been done to their relatives.

Red Buffalo was anxious to get started that morning on building the lodges for our sacred teaching. He explained to me that we had a great deal of work to accomplish. The morning sunlight reflected a dazzling display of green, blue, and violet hues shimmering on the lake surface like a 70's laser light show. Cattails hid the likes of great blue heron, green heron, marsh wren and a multitude of red winged black birds singing in the understory that surrounded the pond at our work site. Flashes of red and yellow darting about reminded me of a Jackson Pollack abstract painting against the cerulean blue of the sky.

We leveled two circular areas of vegetation about sixteen feet across for our stone-people-lodge frameworks about twenty yards from each other on an east to west axis. We dug holes in the center of the two circles in the soil about three feet across and about two feet deep where the heated stones would be placed during the ceremonies. With the material we dug up from those central pits we made elliptical shaped mounds approximately two feet by one foot by around eight inches high just outside the stone-people-lodge circles a few feet away from each lodge entrance. One entrance faced East, and one faced West. These dirt mounds would become the altars where the sacred pipes and any other ceremonial items would rest during the experience. Just a few yards from these mounds, we cleared a larger circle of vegetation approximately eight feet across between the two structures. This area would serve as the central fireplace where we would build our fires to heat up the stones for each lodge.

On each lodge circle that we had drawn in the soil we dug sixteen small holes. These were equidistant from each other, just wide enough to hold our saplings, in the earth. They were positioned approximately 6-8 inches into the soil at an angle away from the center of the circle; 1-2 inches wide. In each of those holes we placed our willow sticks, each approximately sixteen feet high, to be bent towards center at the height a person would sit about four feet tall. After praying above each hole and pinching an offering of tobacco the beginnings of our stone people lodges were then pressed and bent towards the willow on the opposite side of the circle. These were then tied together until we had the look of an upside down basket in place. We then placed other willow saplings around the basket-like framework into the weaving of our side walls. We used twine that we cut into 8 inch strips to tie the frameworks together. After several hours of work for each stone- people-lodge frame of willows, the dome-like structures were completed.

We waited for the night of the ceremony to place the blankets and other tarps over our framework. A thick stick was cut to the size of the door opening and tied on both sides to blankets that would serve as the opening when the time came. Red Buffalo had informed me that in the old days animal hides were utilized for such a structure to hold in the heat. I heard an eagle whistling somewhere in the distance and then saw it come into view and circle over our lodges exactly four times before it disappeared over the ridge as if to put an exclamation point on the magic of my day. Golden eagle sightings in our canyon were rare. We spent the rest of our day stacking the wood and stones for our ceremony near the lodge structures.

That evening, over a picnic of chicken and Carol's potato salad, Black Elk and Spotted Eagle joined us for the teaching. My oldest son gave them his room so they would be comfortable during their stay with us. Red Buffalo and Bill seemed to be thoroughly enjoying the tipi by the pond.

That night Black Elk came out of his room to speak to me in our living room after everyone else had gone to bed. The topic of my Spirit directed education came up and he offered me some unusual advice. He asked me to set aside whatever my formal academic training had covered so as to better understand the direct knowledge I would experience while in the stone- people-lodge ceremonies. It was his opinion that formal education created specific boundaries regarding our perception of reality and he asked me not to restrict my view of their world in any manner. He maintained that I had to be free to "see" from a perspective very different from the average man. He felt our perceiving of reality was usually the direct result of what we had been taught to "see" by family and friends as youngsters. What was possible and impossible was clearly laid out in childhood rather than the "real" that actually existed. He explained to me what his teachers had explained to him, that what most people viewed as reality was really a very limited construct of what actually existed and was possible. He already knew that I did not just see animals, plants, and trees, but that I was beginning to see and feel their presence in many other ways. Though I had not discussed it with anyone I had experienced several levels of what he was alluding to regarding the sacred environment I had become intimate with. His spiritual allies had already informed him of my connection to the spirit realms.

CHAPTER 5
SINGING A NEW MEMORY

The history of the Native Americans living in the canyon now called Wilderness Gardens Preserve, in preceding centuries, was one of migration along the San Luis Rey River and its tributaries in paradise-like temperatures year round. They hunted abundant populations of wildlife throughout the year, while seasonally fishing from the foothill streams and the ocean. They augmented their primary food sources by harvesting acorns in the fall from the massive coast live oak trees that thrived in the canyons. Some of these massive tree structures formed canopies of shade that extended for several acres per tree. The oldest of these were hundreds of years of age and could have contained two dozen men in a group hug at their ground level trunks.

While walking in that wilderness I often felt the presence of the ancient ancestors that had lived there before me. I imagined they had lived an idyllic existence in isolated pockets long after the invasion on the East coast of the Europeans to our shores. Local populations of Luiseno, Serrano, Cahuilla, Cupeno, Kumuyai, Quechan, Cocopa, Papago, Paipai, and the Kiliwa were parts of an extraordinary original people living in the peaceful harmony of this moderate climate and all it had to offer.

I was lost in this thought as I spotted Black Elk walking towards me and waved as I perched on one of my favorite meditation areas the morning after his arrival. An outcropping of granite served as my viewing porch up the slope of our elfin forested canyon, overlooking the valley floor.

At that moment a golden eagle soared past me on the warm thermals in a sky so blue it reminded me of a deep patch of the Pacific Ocean itself. When I questioned him about my eagle sightings including the one that had circled over me four times while constructing the stone-people-lodge Black Elk informed me they were his scouts. Throughout our years of working together one always seemed to arrive before he did. We always joked about it. H said in time I might learn more when I was ready.

The sun's morning light had just streaked above our canyon walls like a crown of jewels shining forth over each rock formation causing her brown tones to take on a golden appearance.

"Ho, Grandson, the lodges look beautiful, thank you for working so hard for our spiritual gathering. He said Spotted Eagle was with Carol and the boys. "Tunkashila woke me this morning with the beauty of those colors from Grandfather Sun."

He reflected for a moment, and then began to talk. "The stones, and the plants, and the trees, and other two-leggeds, and four-leggeds, and the creatures that crawl, and those that fly, could all communicate to each other in the first 'Great Age' of beings on the Earth Mother. They knew about the way of harmony that we have forgotten. We are now at the end of the fourth of these 'Great Ages'. One in which man has attempted to dominate the planet. Each prior Great Age a major earth event has changed the pathway of humanity."

"Each of the *nations of life*, not just the human nations that live on earth, holds a portion of the wisdom left here by Great Spirit. We are each a drop of Great Spirit and very important to the balance of all things."

When I pray with my Chanunpa I am able to communicate with all forms of life. It is like tapping into a unique kind of electrical current. I call it mind talk. This form of telepathy has revealed a great deal of the knowledge I utilize on this pathway. The stone-nation is a perfect example of one of the many other life forms most people disregard. This is a big mistake. The stone-nation has long reminded the Lakota people of how important all life is. The stones are our record keepers and help us in many ways. Their communication and powers are remarkable. Human beings must let go of their spiritual arrogance to connect with the non-human members of our planetary family. They must learn to listen to the many voices of Great Spirit." I knew his last statement was directed squarely at me. I hoped he did not think I was too arrogant for his teachings.

We walked on along the edge of our meadow trail and descended down to the river bottom. It was there that he spoke to me about the language and songs of Mother Earth.

"Grandson, listen to that song… There are many songs in this universe. There are literally countless songs. Take for example, the fire we are going to build for our ceremony tomorrow evening. It has a song. Fire shapes and forms all life. Each shape has a song. The stones you and Bill and Steve picked out yesterday, each have a song. Each one also has a language. The entire Earth Mother also has a song. The water in your river there has a song. This tree we are standing under has a song. There is also a language amongst the trees in this canyon and elsewhere. One man could never know all of the songs. Do you smell that scent in the air? Each one of these trees puts out a particular scent. It acts as a message for other beings like the songs we sing."

"There are many languages in the natural world. That bird has a song. Spirit has gifted me an eagle song, a buffalo song, a whale song, and many other songs. My relatives have passed down many medicine songs to my family. In many cases they fasted four days and four nights to pray and sometimes their efforts were rewarded with a song that would put them in contact with a spirit. Tomorrow will be an opportunity for you to hear some of them." I mentioned that Red Buffalo and Bill had already been teaching me some of them while we worked together.

"When we go to pray in our stone-people-lodges many participants will want help with their problems. So we will sing special songs to help them receive help from the nature spirits. On *Turtle Island,* we could go anywhere and we might find a quiet place and learn a song. We can sit by your river and just enjoy creation. I listen to this bubbling brook and take it into my heart. It becomes a medicine that way. I listen to the wind moving through these massive powerful trees and I am amazed how beautiful it all sounds. Then I listen to all the bird nations here and I fill up on those sounds like a hungry bear cub at his first good meal of spring. I simply enjoy listening to what Spirit might have to say to me through that sound. Let it flow naturally into your heart and mind, Grandson, and it will continue to be a medicine for you. Do not be alarmed by those natural voices. They are very special gifts from Great Spirit."

"The foundation of the way of a wichasa wakan lies in the fire, rock, water, and plant. You have made many deep connections to these nations since becoming a part of these grounds. I am here to help you because of that communication. Red Buffalo has come for the same reason"

We proceeded that day in peaceful silence back to my house and joined our loved ones in preparation for our sacred gathering. I was still working on the entrance parking areas. I was always concerned with fire hazards in the canyon that time of year. Red Buffalo and Black Elk seemed to be catching up on what they each had been up to recently. Spotted Eagle was busy making the spirit robes and prayer ties for the rituals. That evening Black Elk explained to me that the best way to understand what he meant when he spoke of the spirits was to utilize the eye that connects our heart to our mind. He called that connection the third eye and made me aware that the ancients knew true wisdom was gleaned by this connection.

In a moment of quiet we later he explained that he had recently gone to Stanford University and built a stone-people-lodge by one of their labs. They had set up special equipment that had the capability of recording subtle energies around the lodge structure. What they recorded during the ceremony were lights going in and out of the structure. He smiled broadly when he shared that they had caught the movement of Spirit during the ritual.

This pipe filling song is the first ceremonial song that I learned:

> Kola lece lecun wo
> Do it this way my friend
>
> Kola lece lecun wo
> Do it this way my friend
>
> Kola lece lecun wo he
> Do it this way my friend
>
> E canukitaku yacinku ihecetu ktelo
> Your prayer will become reality
>
> Canunpa wanzi yuha elota kecin
> Whenever you sit with the pipe
>
> Minksuya opagi o he
> Always remember me
>
> He canuki ni tunkashila waniang uktelo

CHAPTER 6
WALLACE BLACK ELK SPEAKS

On the afternoon of Black Elk's first public teaching at Wilderness Gardens I could hear the sounds of the summer river play the stones along the stream like a unique other worldly musical instrument. I strolled past some of my favorite boulders along its edges with an emerging appreciation and perspective. The river had beckoned me to her side for a few quiet moments before our gathering began. I remember asking Great Spirit for everything to go successfully throughout our special teaching.

When people began to arrive I was amazed at what a cross section of human beings they were. It seemed we had representatives of all of the human nations. Red, black, brown, yellow, white, young and old, thin and fat, tall and short, political and apolitical, wealthy and poor, were each there that day.

Black Elk's native wisdom lectures and stone-people-lodges had been well received in many places around the world. He had met with such luminaries as Sai Baba from India, Nelson Mandela from South Africa, and the Dalai Lama from Tibet, to discuss different aspects about Native Americans. He had lectured before the United Nations, Geneva Convention, and International Ecumenical Counsel. He had discussed possible solutions to some of the problems Native Americans were having, with President Kennedy, and later Bobby Kennedy, before they were assassinated.

On the other side of that spectrum was Red Buffalo. He had practiced his healing gift in semi-obscurity around the reservations of South Dakota and he seemed shy around those first arriving at Wilderness Gardens . There had been an instant connection between us. It was almost as if we knew each other prior to meeting to begin our work together. He had labored for a bureaucracy as a peace-officer on a reservation in the north part of his State for a time. I wondered if he could relate to me regarding that part of my job. He had explained to me in private that it had been hard on his family when he had made his decision to become an *icshe wichasa*. He now depended on his people to help support him and his family rather than the paycheck he used to receive as a police officer.

He explained that he and Black Elk had discussed my spiritual education and that I should enter his ceremony as my beginning stone- people-lodge, if I was so inclined. He knew that most of the people at the gathering had come for the chance to be in ceremony with Black Elk. Grandfather's lodges would be extremely crowded. Carol and I discussed the possibility of participating together, but she chose to be with our children rather than leave them with a sitter. She participated in many stone-people-lodges, mostly in family settings with me pouring water, in later years.

I heard a distant meadow lark singing just before Black Elk began talking to that assembled body of people. Those seven to ten notes always seemed to have flute-like rhythm to me and were among my favorite bird songs. I thought instantly that hearing that song was a good omen. The canopy of coast live oak trees offered shade for those who needed a rest from the sun. He invited the crowd of around 150 men, women, and children to get comfortable. He urged them to sit down on the meadow grass surrounding the lodges we had constructed by the lake to make contact with our Mother the Earth. As I looked around I viewed a sea of blankets, lawn chairs, and people in various poses on rocks and grass. One man propped himself in the arms of one of our large oak trees.

Black Elk prayed to Grandfather and Grandmother, to the powers of the Animal nations, to the powers of the Four Winds, and he asked for help for the Chanunpa, the Earth, and all beings. He then sang a song. It was an honoring song to the powers that had brought everyone on their safe journey to Wilderness Gardens Preserve. He backed up his singing with the beat of his own double sided elk hide covered drum. It had been stretched over cottonwood about 16 inches across.

Yesterday morning he had been teaching me about songs and the part they play in the symphony of our universe and that message was underlined with the drum beat and the sounds of his words. Over my years of working with him I heard him speak many times. The following is a condensed version of his message that day, and many other days: "Today let us share this beautiful space with the stones, these plants, these trees, the river, the sky, and all of the life forms here. Let us honor the animal nations that are your neighbors. Listen to all of these nations this day. They have power. Great Spirit dwells in all of them. There is power in a tiny ant, a bird, a tree, and a rock. Quiet your minds and listen to the Earth Mother. She is your real mother and Creator is your real father."

"You will need to be patient this day. Slow down and spend some of your time in contemplation. Enjoy the tranquility of this setting. Why are you in such a hurry in your daily lives? You are speeding so fast. Many of you look at your clocks throughout your day and you want time to hurry up. You are wishing your lives away!"

"Feel the other nations here. They are *lela wakan*. There is no English translation for these words. The closest definition in your language would be "beyond sacred". Renew yourselves with their spirits."

"I am an Earth Man—a Lakota, a Man of Peace. We communicate to the rivers, the lakes, to the winds, to the wingeds, to the four-leggeds, to all the other beings of the Earth Mother. When we crawl into our stone-people-lodges later tonight renew yourselves with that steam. Breathe it deeply and utilize it like medicine. And when we smoke the Chanunpa, honor it and all of Creation, and think of your prayers with the intensity of your mind and heart. The Chanunpa is sacred and its use puts you in touch with Creator. Tunkashila said all creatures are my hand. The winged birds are my hand. The four-legged animals are my hand. The fish in the sea and those creatures that crawl are my hand. The two-legged humans are my hand. So watch very carefully. My hand is sacred. When I say to all my relations, o mi takuye oyasin… that is the greatest prayer."

He spoke eloquently about his life. He talked about the sacred mystery powers he had acquired on his own pathway. He made it known that he had experienced what others would call miracles along this pathway, and that our society had really avoided taking a look at those because they seemed unexplainable. He emphasized that people had been cured of some of society's worst diseases in the stone-people-lodge by Great Spirit. He explained *hanbleycha*, the Lakota version of a "vision quest". He related several stories of his no food or water experiences, up on the mountains where his hanbleychas had taken place. He shared how he talked to powerful spirit beings during that sacred time on many occasions.

He spoke to the crowd about the *Sun Dance*, another powerful sacred ritual performed over four days of dancing under the Sun and connecting to a forked tree with a rope attached to skewers inserted into the skin of his chest and breaking free. He let them know how much he had learned about the universe in that sacred circle. He let them know he ran a Sun Dance up in the Ashland area of Oregon that allowed all skin colors to participate. Many Sun Dances were not this way. Also purification stone-people-lodge ceremonies were discussed and he invited anyone to participate after the lecture. He let everyone know there was no charge for that part of our time together. His lectures were structured like circles as are many important cycles of life. He would usually circle back to the main thought that all things are sacred on the planet and because of this we should respect each other before we destroy ourselves. "Nineteen generations ago there was a great meeting of the people of Turtle Island. At that time everyone spoke the same language. The purpose of that gathering was to assure that everyone understood the sacred ceremonies through which men and women could communicate in a sacred manner with all their relations. At that time the people were instructed to come together every seventh generation to reaffirm their understanding. It was agreed that counsel would continue until everyone understood completely. After the third Counsel, prophesies foretold that in the fifth generation tremendous dissonance would prevail upon the earth. Eventually the use of the Chanunpa would save the planet from disaster."

After our break in the lecture Red Buffalo set up his family drum. It was a double sided buffalo covered instrument approximately 16 inches high by about 3 feet across with a picture of a buffalo painted on its surface. It was placed on wooden blocks and he and Bill and another helper sang for the assembled group several ancient songs.

Black Elks wife, Grace Spotted Eagle, then spoke very eloquently to the group from a feminine perspective on her view of the "Sacred Way". She explained that she felt now more than ever before on the planet, a feminine balance was needed to help protect the other nations that lived with human beings. She explained that our lack of regard for the animal nations, the plant nations, and the mineral nations had put us humans in a very precarious position on the Earth Mother. She believed it was time for women to take their proper place in leadership roles to help with the great healing process in whatever peaceful way their spiritual guides advised. Since walking by Black Elk's side for many years, she had attended many of his purification lodges as his sacred singer to call in the special helpers-the spirits that assisted in this work. She too had seen many examples of the "great mystery powers" and had experienced the powers first hand. She explained that in her own culture it was the women who usually prepared the tobacco offerings, "*prayer ties*" for the wichasa wakan who would be pouring water for the inipi ceremony. She added that each person could ask for specific help from the spirits by utilizing a pinch of tobacco-putting a prayer in the tobacco, and literally tying that thought within a colored piece of cotton cloth about an inch squared. Creating a string of these thoughts in each little pouch and hanging those ties within the stone-people-lodge was a serious matter . She informed the group she usually tied 150 red prayer ties for Black Elks ceremonies on one string. In these she included prayers for health and help. He would usually ask for specific help with the other colors if appropriate on another string. She mentioned for us to speak with her when we did our prayer ties and she would instruct each of us on proper color selection.

Spotted Eagle went on to explain that in each direction, North , East, South, and West, during Black Elk's ceremonies, she hung a *spirit robe* to honor the powers of those directions. Those robes could vary a bit in size, but she liked to make them around 2-3 feet in length and 6-8 inches wide. A prayer with a larger pinch of tobacco was placed in one corner of each of those. She explained that around the time of Grandfather Nicholas Black Elk's work the wichasa wakans were allowed to switch from spirit robes and prayer ties made from colored animal hides to spirit robes and prayer ties made from cotton cloth. She explained that a finding ceremony was completed in those ancient years to find the colored rocks to make the colors for the hides. This was completed at night and the stones would glow to those collecting them. She also mentioned to the women that anyone on their moon time-menses, should realize they are already in a phase of purification with the Great Mother, and should honor the wichasa wakan's request that they not participate in the lodges at that time.

Because we were in a canyon the gloaming darkness usually arrived earlier than on the flatlands above the park. During this time Dr. William Lyon explained how the listeners would be divided into groups of approximately thirty people to participate in the stone-people-lodges.

He explained that everyone would need to be patient and quiet during the lodges that would take place while they waited their turn to crawl in. While he spoke I helped Bill and a few of Black Elks assistants cover each lodge first with a layer of blankets, then a layer of thick black plastic. This material was used instead of the hides from their history to keep the heat inside. We attached ropes on each side of a horizontal stick that held a thick blanket that would serve as a door for each lodge. The ropes were then extended to the opposite sides of the igloo looking structures and secured to large stones to hold them in place. The stones that were chosen to be part of the ceremony were then prayed over, and put into the sacred fire pit on four logs that ran East to West and four on top of those that ran North to South. These formed the base for the fire. These were surrounded by four foot sections of split wood and kindling which we prayed over and then lit. After what seemed like about an hour and a half the stones took on the color of a bright red orange peel.

CHAPTER 7
SEVEN SACRED FIRES

At this point in the evening Black Elk and Red Buffalo sat quietly in a meditative state by the lodges they would enter shortly. Each shaman had informed their helpers tending the fire how many stones they would require. This number varied from ceremony to ceremony based on the instructions from their spiritual allies regarding what they were trying to accomplish during each ritual.

Tipis stood tall and regal in the meadow between our lakes. They were decorated with eagle feathers that vibrated in the light breeze as if we had gone back in time to a native scene recorded by a George Catlin painting. The first groups of stone-people-lodge participants utilized the tipis to change into comfortable lodge wear. Black Elk felt that to keep peoples' minds properly focused, light weight cotton clothing or bathing suits were encouraged at mixed gender ceremonies. At other single gender gatherings, clothing was optional. The wichasa wakan in charge of a ceremony always crawled into the lodge enclosure first, followed by the women and children. The men usually went in last. People were reminded to leave anything metal out of the lodge and to crawl around the central pit that would house the stones like a birds nest. All movements were carried out in a *sun-wise*, "clockwise" manner. Participants lined up outside the lodges they had been assigned to attend. The sacred fire between both lodges blazed long into that night. As I viewed the scene, it looked as if sparks were flying to the stars on wings of an invisible wind. The stars reflected in the lake were shattered into tiny bits of light as children wandered along its border.

Some participants brought tobacco offerings to the shaman they would work with that evening. These could be presented with requests for specific help or knowledge. If those asking for help were Chanunpa-carriers, they filled their Chanunpas and presented them four times to a shaman. Then they stated their requests. Black Elk and Red Buffalo would wait with outstretched arms. They would reach palms up and accept or reject the Chanunpas based on input from their spiritual allies. If the request was accepted, on the fourth pass the Chanunpa was taken and it became part of the spiritual agenda within the stone-people-lodge that evening.

As we prepared to go into the lodges, Black Elk instructed that this was the best time to do healing work because of the balance of sun and moon as the last light dissipated. He and Red Buffalo allowed both male and female participants into each ceremony. They clarified that some families participated separately by gender.

Red Buffalo crawled into our lodge and sat to the right of the opening that would be covered by blankets to create the door. I could see Black Elk doing the same at his lodge. We were shoulder to shoulder inside the lodge in two concentric circles in lodges that faced each other perhaps fifty feet apart on an East and West axis. I settled into position right next to the stones in the inner circle of Red Buffalos lodge. From my vantage point I could see the firemen working hard with the wood, stones, and fire outside of the lodges in the central fire pit. They were sweating profusely glistening with red-orange firelight reflected on their features. The stones were dusted with cedar branches so few ashes were brought into the enclosures. Once inside, they were blessed with sage and sweet grass by a motion of touching each stone with each medicine. The first seven stones were touched with the wooden mouth piece of the Chanunpa as well. *Cha-sha-sha*, "the smoking mixture" made up of tobacco and non-hallucinogenic herbs, had been filled prior to going into the ceremony. The Chanunpas were placed on the earthen mounds utilized as altars, just outside each lodge door with their stems pointing west. The stones were brought into our enclosure via pitch fork. After they were placed in the central pit within the lodges they were further positioned with two deer antlers by a helper inside the lodge. Seven stones came in to begin our ceremony. These were followed by four more. It was already extremely hot in that front row. The red hot stones were approximately twelve inches from my body. Red Buffalo had prepared me for this and had recommended I bring in my towel to protect my legs. I was grateful for his advice as the temperature grew fierce almost immediately.

Red Buffalos' singer sat next to the fireman who was positioned nearest the door on the left. The ceremonial singer is integral to the success of each ceremony. He or she is asked to sing the songs requested by the wichasa wakan during each segment of the ritual . Because a singer was not always available a wichasa wakan needed to at times handle both responsibilities. In most ceremonies the fireman would be the last person to crawl in after he had carried out any last minute requests by the shaman in charge. It was the fireman's responsibility to bring in the water that would be poured over each stone via a water bucket and wooden ladle.

As I looked around our enclosure I could see many faces around our circle exhibiting a nervous anticipation. Others closed their eyes in prayer. As I sat in silence I stared at the sacred fire outside our lodge flickering then as if someone was turning the lights on and off. Red Buffalo then asked for the door blankets to be dropped into place. When this was accomplished, the only light was that reflected from the red hot stones. When the door closed I could feel the temperature rise again from my front row seat. I could see faces in the shadows of the red stones. Once the water began to be poured, those same faces disappeared into the pitch black space of that inside world. I could hear Black Elk begin his ceremony in the other sweat-lodge and then his voice trailed off.

"We have put the heat of Tunkashila, Grandfather Spirit, back inside of these stone-people. These ancient ones are wise and will assist me in my work here", Red Buffalo stated quite seriously. He began our ceremony with a prayer and brief instructions. He always stated that if anyone needed to leave the circle, just say *mitakuye oyasin*, or "to all my relations", and the fireman would open the blanket flap to the air and that person's eventual exit. He spoke English to let people know how we would proceed. Most of the rest of the ceremony was completed using the Lakota language-with a few English explanations. The heat grew in intensity as the first four songs were sung. During this segment Red Buffalo explained we were back in the womb of our real Mother-the Earth. I could sense how powerful the *inyan,* "stones" had become. The enclosure filled with steam. It grew extremely hot. I wondered if I could endure the temperature. Then another level of awareness an octave above normal took hold of me. Red Buffalo asked us to breathe the steam like it was a medicine to purify our contaminated bodies. I prayed hard for my family and everyone there. After the singing, to the major relief of many participants, Red Buffalo asked for the door to be opened. Sweat seemed to run out of every pore. The fresh air felt exhilarating. The fireman was asked to fan several people with Red Buffalo's eagle feather fan. It seemed to revive them almost immediately.

Soon after the lodge was allowed to fill with fresh air, and the next seven stones were brought into the enclosure. Moments after we began the singing in the second segment of our ceremony, I viewed several bright white lights, approximately six to eight inches round, floating high above us. I changed my perspective several times to verify they were not optical illusions. After the songs requested were completed, the prayer segment of our ceremony began from the outer circle to the inner circle. Most prayers were emotional and heartfelt. It remained extremely hot throughout the prayer segment. I found I had no idea how much ordinary time had passed before the door opened and we smoked the Chanunpa. I could hear the stones hissing as we passed around the pipe. Because of the large gathering of people waiting, the usual four segments of the ceremony were reduced to two. We were instructed, that as we smoked, we should hold our prayers in our minds and hearts. When

I crawled out I felt oddly exhilarated. The sage, cedar, and sweet grass that Red Buffalo utilized, were considered spiritual allies and quite helpful in the purification process. "The plant-people have long been utilized as a cleansing medicine by my people," he told the participants. Smoking embers could be seen in the abalone shell on the altar outside our lodge as we departed. His Chanunpa was taken apart after everyone that participated had smoked it and it was left on the altar outside the lodge until it would be filled again for the next ceremony. The area between each altar and sacred fire was restricted to firemen and shaman once the Chanunpas were in place. Pipe filling songs prior to each ceremony during the filling of the Chanunpas always took place as a way of honoring the sacred pipes.

Healing in different forms occurred throughout the night. Red Buffalo gave some of the people that had asked for help instructions during the ceremony. He explained these came from his *spiritual allies*. Others received their instructions immediately afterwards in conferences with Red Buffalo by the lodge. While this was taking place I sat in silence by our pond taking in what might have been viewed by some as a flashback to an ancient encampment. I found it remarkable how patient people were throughout the night.

After checking with Red Buffalo, he squeezed me into his third stone-people-lodge later that night. When one ceremony was completed another set of stones were heated and another group began their participation. Most people did not want to leave the area. There were many on the perimeter of the light from the sacred fire in deep meditation and awe from what had transpired. Others wandered off to their camp sites or out to their vehicles at the park entrance.

During Red Buffalos final ceremony of the night I entered the lodge just before his singer. I experienced my second stone-people-lodge from the back row of what were also two concentric circles of participants. His instructions were nearly the same as in our first lodge of the evening with a few exceptions for specific people who had made requests of him. I felt a little more at ease. The heat was hotter than a central valley afternoon in the heart of summer by many degrees. When his singer began the second segment of the ceremony after the door had been closed to the soothing evening air, something touched my back. I knew my back was near the blanketed lodge structure, however, this was very different. It then touched my face and heart, softly blessing me. I could hear bird wings flapping above me now in the lodge and my sensation was that I had been touched by those wings. I felt the feathers specifically. No one else had moved. I wondered what else might await me in that deep space. When I peered into the darkness of that black light I saw the red and blue shapes of birds flying in the top portion of the lodge. They seemed ethereal. Then they disappeared. When we crawled out I should have felt exhausted from our day yet I felt exhilarated. I found another quiet spot underneath several oak trees to help me process what had just occurred. The skeptic in me wondered about the feathers and sounds within that structure. I then realized I had reached out just after I had the sensations and there was only air. The person directly in front of me had felt nothing after I asked him specifically afterwards. Those observations emphasized what Red Buffalo and Black Elk had explained that each participant experienced various aspects of the phenomenon in a unique way.

Red Buffalo and I eventually crawled into Black Elk's last inipi ceremony. It was made up of singers and helpers. It ended as the sun was rising. I was impressed that Black Elk had poured water for four ceremonies. Red Buffalo had poured for three and was now participating again to help with the singing. Spotted Eagle sang the sacred songs throughout the night. She was one tough Grandmother. I took note of her precise drum beats and pleasing voice as I settled into the first segment of his ceremony. I attended three stone-people-lodge ceremonies that evening. I surprised myself by this action. During Black Elk's ceremony the heat was the most intense for me that night. I was again stationed in the front row of his lodge and felt like my normal awareness had been moved to a higher octave during the proceedings. He had explained to me the previous day that what we felt temperature wise was not always a direct correlation to the physical heat inside the structure. Someone working on a major healing or specific request could feel more heat than someone sitting right next to them. During the final segment of each of the ceremonies water was passed to any participant that wanted it. People were always advised if they needed to leave to let him know. After the singing and during the prayers I saw what Black Elk explained to me afterward were what appeared to be tiny lightning's bouncing around the stones. I viewed them for several minutes and then they disappeared into the depths of the sheer blackness where I could not even see my hand in front of my face. He explained to me they came to help with whatever healing had been requested. During the last segment of songs the earth seemed to be vibrating under me. Each wichasa wakan's courage, endurance, alertness, and love for others seemed truly remarkable.

They told me the following day, "That Spirit had come to help many people that evening in that gathering." They were not bragging. They were simply stating a fact.

I had no more sweat or energy to give when I crawled out of Black Elk's lodge as the sun was about to rise! I wandered down the trail to my house quite dazzled by it all. I felt like a crystal that had been cleaned off and was once again gleaming. I found myself perfectly able to "see" in the way my new path would require. Both of my icshe wichasa teachers had each known of my discovery prior to me telling them. Approximately twenty-four hours later they each sat down with me to what in my later years I would consider a teaching session regarding the events of our time together.

They informed me that an eagle spirit had blessed me with his feathers. I was told this was a good sign for things to come.

CHAPTER 8
IN TWO WORLDS I WALK

My shamanic education began to accelerate as the days, weeks, and months flowed by me, following those initial ceremonies with Black Elk and Red Buffalo. Even the number of our sacred rituals that night was significant from my new perspective. Our seven sacred fires somehow made more sense in light of the Seven Lakota Council Fires that had roamed as nomadic tribes during their days of freedom on the Great Plains. The number seven was significant to a wichasa wakan also for the number of energies brought into the sacred pipe for help before each ritual. These were the powers of each of the four directions: North, *tatanka oyate*, "buffalo nation", East, *hehaka oyate*, "deer nation", South, *wamakashka oyate*, "all other nations", West, *wakinyan oyate*, "thunder beings", Wakan Tanka, "father sky", *unshi maka*, "earth mother", and *wanbli oyate*, "eagle nation". The number seven was associated with good fortune. The number four was also revered by the Lakota for its connection to the four seasons and the *powers of the four winds*, "time and space".

I incorporated similar gatherings for Black Elk and Spotted Eagle, and Red Buffalo and his wife Pam, in what became a unique teaching program for the community and region. Participants from these events made it known to me that their lives had changed in many powerful ways. I became even more intrigued by it all. Black Elk and Red Buffalo had presented me with an eagle feather after our initial teaching sessions and explained how

I could utilize the feather like a Chanunpa when I prayed in my ceremonies. They encouraged me to accomplish some stone-people-lodge ceremonies for my family and friends. Though I was hesitant at first, over the months that followed, I eventually felt quite comfortable pouring water and praying with my eagle feather at what became extremely important knowledge acquisition sessions for me.

When Grandfather Black Elk and Red Buffalo returned to the Preserve I was asked to perform the duty of fireman for each shaman at their public gatherings. Black Elk instructed, "The fire spirits will continue your education in many ways." It was at these fires that I developed an even deeper connection to the stones that I collected in the wild and prayed over. Grandfather Black Elk emphasized, "If a person has the ears to hear the stone spirits will divulge great wisdom. Fire itself is one of the primary gifts from *Wakan Tanka* . Red Buffalo explained to me, "There will come a time when you build the pyramid of stones covered with sticks in the fire pit and it will light on its own without a match." This happened on more than one occasion in my history of fire tending for them.

I was beginning to assimilate each new experience from my "Sacred Way" perspective. Leaving my intellectual attitudes behind was difficult. Black Elk and Red Buffalo often sought information to help a person with their shamanic skills acquired over many years of arduous practice. I felt incredibly fortunate to have them each sharing so much of their own knowledge to help further my own progress on my path. Though their conversations with those that requested healing were private, I was aware that people were asking for help with serious ailments as well as minor ones. Some of these people were advised they needed to accomplish further work in future ceremonies. These often included four healing stone-people-lodges on four future nights. Other times one ceremony was all that was required by their spiritual helpers to accomplish the work. On other occasions something specific was requested in the way of an herb or other sacred implement. If a complete curing was not possible, sometimes a healing of a lesser degree could take place to reduce pain or discomfort. Many claimed to be cured of very serious ailments after accomplishing what was requested by Spirit.

Black Elk and Spotted Eagle taught me many songs to be utilized in my own ceremonies during that phase of my training. Red Buffalo did the same.

A sacred man's altar during an inipi is defined by how he presents his spirit-robes. These are the rectangular shaped pieces of cotton cloth tied in one corner with a tobacco pouch prayer. These are hung like flags within the lodge from each of the four cardinal directions. Prayer-ties are also part of a specific altar presentation at each ceremony varying in color and the amount of prayer-ties. Also considered part of a wichasa wakan's altar were any special stones, feathers, rattles, fans, or other personal implements of power to connect him to his spiritual allies. I grew particularly fascinated by the colors of the spirit-robes and prayer-ties my teachers had so benevolently shared with me. They explained that red, yellow, white, and black, were utilized to bring the spiritual powers of the four winds to that specific location. They also utilized green and blue for certain ceremonies often related to Sun Dance. These spirit robes were hung between the black and the red spirit-robes in this altar. Green represented Mother Earth and could be utilized to acquire a plant medicine in a healing ceremony. Blue represented Wakan Tanka, Great Spirit, and was utilized to acquire knowledge for a specific purpose.

Many cultures consider these principle four colors to be references back to the beginning races of human beings. I was surprised when I discovered that medicine people around the world utilized similar systems when asking for their help. Shamans in the Southwest utilize those colors and relate them to the four principle colors of their sacred corn. Shamans in Egypt utilize those colors in their astrology and alchemy practices. The Taoist philosophers of ancient China and Japan utilized them. They were also utilized in the prayer flags of Tibet. Aboriginal shamans in Australia utilize them and relate them to the four principle colors of their soils. Even our modern day astronomers utilize them to designate the four principle phases in the lives of stars. These are red giants, yellow suns, white dwarves, and black holes. I believe this was what Grandfather Black Elk meant when he told me he was "teaching me a universal language".

I had been taken under their wings, and advised to view their teachings regarding the Sacred Path from all directions. It seemed to me that a wichasa wakan prayed to the same God I was taught to pray to in my formative years. They had learned to utilize their spirit helpers to assist beings in many ways. I remember thinking to myself that those spirits seemed to be an extension of Gods own hands.

I had walked away from organized religion at the tender age of twelve years after an overly zealous Sunday school teacher had announced during one such session that my own father would most certainly be "going to hell" because he had to work a second job on Sundays to help our family survive. That kind of dogmatic teaching seemed utterly ridiculous-even to a child, and so I worked out some boundaries with my mother back then that when she and my sisters went to church, I would be allowed to go over to my Grandmother's house.

In my beginning days I occasionally slipped back into my western view of where I had been and where I was going. I became fascinated with the mysterious physics of it all. Einstein had suggested that one underlying field existed as the background for all transformations of space, time, mass, and energy. This implies a level of nature that is totally fused. He spent the last thirty years of his life trying to prove a unified field theory. If waking, sleeping, and dreaming, were the major components of our reality, I wondered if the path of a shaman connected to a fourth level. Perhaps in an octave above those three there was actually another state of reality. Einstein's unified field theory connected them all. I felt that the energies a shaman was in touch with were extremely powerful. It was hidden to all except a mind that is able to transcend ordinary activity. Like the focus of a shaman during a stone-people-lodge where the heat, the songs, and the total darkness moves them through the first levels to the fourth. I wondered if their altered consciousness allowed them to reach the fourth level spoken of as a unified field of information. Could the healing a shaman facilitates, with the help of Spirit, connect to this hidden blue print of nature?

They were not successful every time regarding major healing requests. Certain factors beyond our understanding and control would obviously play a role at times. Therefore, I concluded that appropriate mechanisms must click in each time-such as belief, to reach the pure infinite consciousness necessary for success. If Wakan Tanka allowed for a new cause, then there could exist a new effect.

PRAYER-TIES CHART

The following is a condensed chart on the information Black Elk, Red Buffalo, and Spotted Eagle taught me during my training regarding the very intentional and specific action of putting ones prayers into physical reality from our thoughts during these ceremonies:

For health in your home, family, or someone that needs help, or yourself: make one red spirit-robe 2-3 feet in length by 6 inches wide from cotton cloth, also tie 50 red prayer-ties.

For help with your needs in your family, or yourself: make one yellow spirit-robe 2-3 feet in length by 6 inches wide from cotton cloth, also tie 50 yellow prayer-ties.

For thank you when your prayers come to reality: make one white spirit- robe 2-3 feet in length by 6 inches wide from cotton cloth, also tie 50 white prayer-ties.

For understanding for knowledge: make one blue spirit-robe 2-3 feet in length by 6 inches wide from cotton cloth: also tie 75 blue prayer-ties.

For use of medicine make one green spirit-robe 2-3 feet in length and 6 inches wide from cotton cloth, also tie 50 green prayer-ties.

For protection in your home, family, and yourself in everyday life: make one black spirit-robe 2-3 feet in length by 6 inches wide from cotton cloth, also tie 40 black prayer-ties.

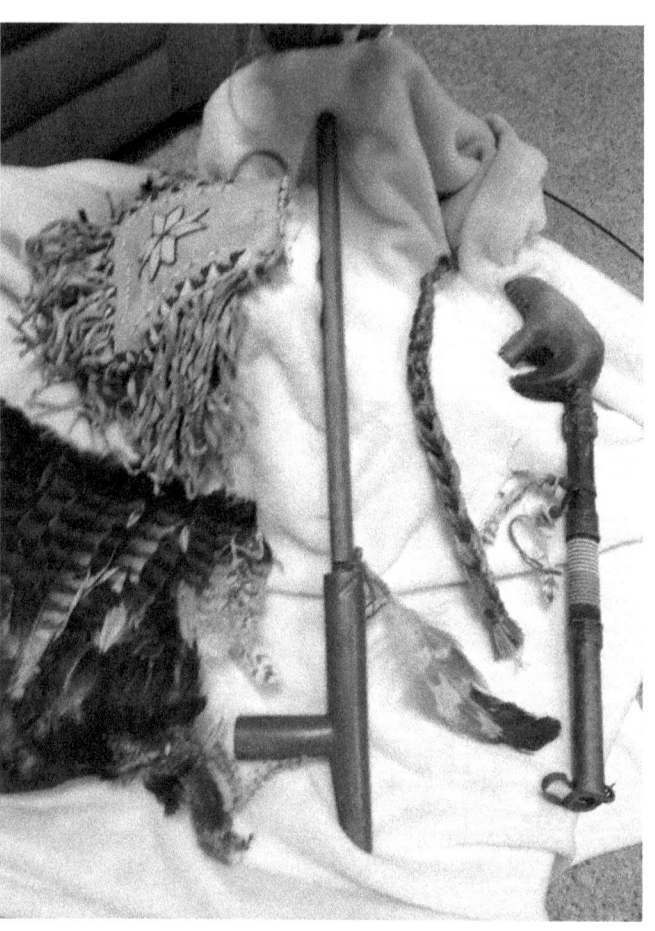

CHAPTER 9
THE SACRED PIPE-CHANUNPA

On subsequent visits my wichasa wakan teachers continued to share thoughts, concepts, and practices that had been passed down to others like them since the Lakota had been placed at the center of Turtle Island in what our historians call pre-history . On these occasions I was put in direct contact with a reality where paranormal energies could sometimes be seen, or heard, or smelled. Miraculous healing and knowledge acquisition were sometimes the results of their efforts. It seemed as though we were breaking through some sort of dimensional barrier where limitations existed in our normal world, to another realm where conceptual distinctions could be accomplished in perfect freedom with a perfectly formed thought.

Because Black Elk lived in Denver, Colorado, and Red Buffalo lived on the Yankton Reservation, on the eastern side of South Dakota, it was special to have them together in my area of the world. These occasions were filled with new teaching and much laughter. I always stayed in contact via telephone with each man through this stage of my development. I saw more of Grandfather Black Elk because of his extensive lecture schedule across North America and Europe. If he was anywhere close by in those years we often managed to work out some time to share talking or discussing something new I was beginning to experience.

Black Elk and Red Buffalo were more serious than I had ever seen them when they arrived for this particular family stone-people-lodge ceremony. I had been asked to perform the duties of the fireman by Red Buffalo. He explained that both he and Black Elk would be pouring the water over the stones that night. They shared those responsibilities as if they were one shaman. Each poured water during different parts of our four segments that evening. I had never seen or heard of that happening during a ceremony.

In a relatively short time I had become adept at building the fires for their ceremonies. I found a great joy in mastering all aspects of what a fireman accomplished. Because I had spent many years building fires in my own stone home without another heat source, it all felt quite natural to me. It took me a longer time mastering the art of reaching for the stones during a ceremony in a red hot fire ring without scorching myself. Then balancing the stones on a pitchfork and sliding them effortlessly into the lodges without dropping them or piercing someone became commonplace. If a stone was dropped I learned it always went back into the fire to be purified again for future selection. I found that throughout a night of ceremony being a fireman took quite a bit of physical strength and endurance. I undoubtedly became more physically fit from this role. After removing each stone from the fire it is also the fireman's responsibility to dust off the ashes with a cedar bough so lodge participants will not have to breathe smoky air. A fireman who was not thorough in this regard could cause great disruption to the ritual. I was also responsible for moving in and out of the lodges as required to get something off of the altar requested by the shaman for use inside. If a person was in need of doctoring with a feather fan that also was often considered my service at the shaman's request to fan them using a specific motion of the feathers. Filling the water bucket and managing that water both during and after a ceremony were also the humble chores of a fireman. Many a night after a ceremony I spent ladling water to participants that needed a drink. Lighting the Chanunpas whenever they were going to be shared by the participants also fell into my realm of service. If this was not accomplished thoroughly it also could cause problems for all the ceremonial participants with the Chanunpa not staying lit. "A wichasa wakan learns many aspects of his walk observing and handling a fire", Red Buffalo stated.

When they asked me to talk with them privately after everyone else had gone to bed after a searing and steamy four door ceremony I wondered what my next teaching would entail.

Black Elk being the eldest wichasa wakan did most of the talking that evening: "You have been very observant since we began to share with you the sacred ways of the Earth People. You have now experienced many of the powers of this way of life in a very short period of time. We have been advised to proceed with you in this matter. I have lived with these powers all of my life and yet I am in awe of the great mystery they hold. Sometimes I am fearful because of how immense these powers are. However, with the help of *Wakan Tanka,* I am able to put those fears aside. You must do the same if you are to progress. Red Buffalo and I agree you are ready for your next step in these spiritual matters. What we will speak to you about this evening is a very serious matter." Black Elk's eyes seemed to pierce right through mine like a laser through a wall. I could feel my heart begin to pound in a rapid beat. It reminded me of the drumbeat I had utilized that evening.

"At the center of this path we have taught you, is the most sacred implement available to an ikche wichasa. You have seen it at every ceremony we have accomplished together. It is our Chanunpa. The original Chanunpa Wakan was brought to our people through a Spirit. She came out of a cloud, which then turned into a hill. She walked in the shape of a white buffalo. She then became a beautiful maiden dressed in white buckskin. Her name was Ptesan Win. She was discovered by two warriors in that past age, and she asked to appear before that entire group of Earth People. She had in her hands the stone bowl of the Chanunpa, and its wood stem, and a bundle of sage. She told the people that the Chanunpa was sacred and that its proper use would allow a person to connect themselves from the Earth Mother all the way to Wakan Tanka. She explained to them that she had been sent by the buffalo nation to instruct them in the ways of Great Spirit. The human body, mind, and spirit became a sacred link to the above. She taught them to respect all things on the circle of life and showed them how to use that sacred implement. Currently a chosen Lakota family protects that ancient Chanunpa Wakan and it is one of our most cherished artifacts. It is lela wakan. Lela wakan does not translate into English but it is the highest aspect of sacred. The old people say that when she walked away she turned into a deer, then an elk, then a white buffalo, and then disappeared on the horizon."

"There have been three different uses of the Chanunpa amongst my people. One was for social purposes when a pipe was filled and smoked with friends to honor that occasion. Another was a sacred pipe filled as a personal tool to talk with the spirits. The third is utilized by a wichasa wakan in his practice of the old ways to help other beings."

"There are also three ways a Chanunpa is acquired by a human being: The first is through a Spirit. The original Chanunpa Wakan came that way and I have seen others come through a Spirit in ceremony. They manifested before someone in the stone-people-lodges. The second is a wichasa wakan is directed by a Spirit to offer a Chanunpa to someone who is ready to carry such a device to help others. It takes courage, endurance, alertness, and love to be a Chanunpa-carrier. The third is a person has a dream about carrying a Chanunpa and they fulfill that dream by making their own pipe or someone helps them make it."

"That third way was how I received my first Chanunpa. Would you like to hear that story?" The words were hardly out of his mouth as I nodded my head without speaking a word. He collected his thoughts for several minutes and then he began: "First my Grandpa and I went looking for some ash wood for the making of the stem of my pipe in a dry creek bed. He told me I needed to use my intuition after praying about it. I had a straight piece of wood in my mind and heart that was about eighteen inches to two feet long when I began my search. I looked at many ash trees from each direction until after studying one tree I found the piece that I thought could work. I took my Grandpa to that tree and I had him look from the four directions, until he also saw the branch I had selected."

"He filled his Chanunpa at the base of the tree and we smoked it for help in securing that stick. We then sprinkled tobacco around that tree as an outward sign of honoring its spirit and at that time I assumed we would begin to cut it. But Grandpa said we would come back and get it later. Pretty soon four seasons had passed."

"When we went back to that tree all the other branches had new growth coming out of similar branches but not the one I selected. So he was pleased about that and he filled his Chanunpa and we thanked Spirit and went home again for four seasons."

"When we went to that tree again we prayed and this time we cut that perfectly straight branch out of that tree after asking its Spirit for permission. Before we left, Grandpa notched the end of that stick and put an insect he picked off of another branch and he plugged that notch with some green from that tree. Before long that insect had worked its way to the other side of that straight stick! I then stacked it in the middle of some other wood I had collected to keep it from twisting as it dried. It stayed that way for four more seasons."

"That next year we took a trip to Pipestone, Minnesota, where we hoped to collect a piece of catlinite for the base of my pipe. We worked for eight days braking through a top layer of granite to finally find just the right piece of stone that we had prayed about and then we took that piece of stone home. After we cut an elbow shape out of it we used willows, buffalo grease, and ashes to work a hole in it to match the one in my stem. I then shaped it and polished it. In all it took me sixteen seasons to make my Chanunpa. Spirit has connected me to all beings with this sacred tool. It is a pathway you never leave if you are dedicated." Grandfather Black Elk seemed to be investigating my soul at this point in our conversation. There were several minutes of silence.

Then Red Buffalo began to speak: "So cha means wood. Nunpa means two. These form our Tree Of Life. When we put our smoking mixture inside it, the Chanunpa represents the universe-both male and female-stem and base. As we fill it we keep a very clear mind and heart. We ask for help from the powers of the four directions, Father Sky, and Mother Earth. Then we ask the eagle-nation for help in taking our thoughts to Creator." He then took out a simple plain ash wood stem approximately fifteen inches long, and a catlinite base approximately seven inches long by about four inches high and held them in his hands.

"If you choose to honor this path and help others when your own spiritual allies advise it so, Spirit has told us that this Chanunpa I am holding is for you!"

It was all I could do to hold back my tears. I was humbled and at the same time very happy that they thought I was ready for such a responsibility. I accepted my own Chanunpa in that moment from them. I would find out much later the stem had come from Red Buffalo and the base had come from Black Elk. After an extended silence we each returned to our sleeping quarters and I tried to get some sleep. After several hours of contemplation I dropped off into my dreamtime.

The next morning they talked to me about how to care for my Chanunpa properly. Spotted Eagle gave me a piece of hide and a cloth to wrap it in the following day. Black Elk proceeded to inform me that my Chanunpa would need cleaning from time to time. He showed me how a wire could be placed and pulled through it. He further explained how he rubbed animal grease into both the wood and stone to keep it from drying out. He further instructed me about the mixture of the plants that were smoked inside it, which he called chashasha. He explained to me its main ingredient was the bark of a dogwood tree, collected before the first snow. He went on that it was often called red willow by his people. This and several other plants were added to the mixture which varied slightly from place to place. He added that a small quantity of natural tobacco was always added to keep it lit in ceremony. He stated that he used to make his own mixture, but that now he had it made by people where the plants could be acquired easily. He then gave me my first quantity of that smoking mixture and I filled it as they instructed and smoked it with them. He reviewed that the plant material in the mixture represented all parts of the universe. I thanked all the nature spirits where I lived for their help in teaching me during my first prayer with my newly acquired Chanunpa. The ways of the wichasa wakan felt comfortable to me.

They seemed much more truthful and pure than those coming from our modern day religions.

The pathway of a Chanunpa-carrier opened up before me like the magical entrance to a mountain cave. Since that original teaching it has remained incredibly powerful whenever I have put it to use. A person who is able to connect their mind and their heart as they connect their Chanunpas, holds the key to this sacred device. I had been asked to become someone who could call up that special feeling, emotion, and intention necessary to help facilitate a healing or seeing to do Great Spirits work. I felt the burden of such a weight almost immediately.

CHAPTER 10
SPIRITUAL AWAKENING

During my years of learning to walk as a sacred man, Wallace Black Elk and Steve Red Buffalo shared their knowledge with me in many environments. That education took place in areas that were natural and also places as simple as a local restaurant or mall. We walked on beaches, up mountains, in meadows, along stream beds, in forests, and many other places where some other piece to this path was revealed.

When Grace Spotted Eagle passed over, I realized even more how much she had meant to Black

Elk's teaching. He had called her his half-side, and I saw how he naturally struggled to find his balance after her death. She and Grandfather taught me how to properly play my drum in a very short time span. She shared many of the stone-people-lodge songs that I would utilize in my own ceremonies. After she became ill with her cancer, Black Elk tried to help her with a four day ceremony prior to one of his visits to my park. I realized there were instances when the higher powers would not allow a curing to take place.

However, a healing of some partial nature of mind or spirit could also be very important to a patient. Sometimes a cancer victim would not experience the usual symptoms of pain after this kind of work, or they would be allowed a longer walk on the Earth Mother. In Spotted Eagles case the cancer was too advanced to cure and she passed away the following year. I missed her too.

In my families years along the San Luis Rey River, the winter rainy season brought torrents of water that flashed down the canyons to the sea a few miles away. The waters would raise so high and so fast that the bridge to our little stone and brick house became impassable on several occasions. In those instances we were isolated from the world and hidden away in our very private magical oak woodland. Those times became special for our family. Grandfather called winter the *"looks within time"*. He said he always felt it was a time to examine our place in the universe.

In the summer season the character of the river's waters did a complete flip-flop. Sometimes the river disappeared entirely from view under the sweltering sun and mostly appeared as a meandering creek to offer our wild animal population meager nourishment along its edges. Even in that heat we were able to view many creatures in that natural world. My children's love for the animal nations blossomed, and mine continued to expand. We cared for a mollucan cockatoo, an African parrot, several canaries, many turtles, frogs, snakes, guinea pigs, hamsters, exotic fish, chickens, cats, and dogs. Because I volunteered my services to a regional wildlife rehabilitation organization we also cared for roadrunners, ravens, owls, hawks, and even an eagle. The wild animals were loved dearly until we could release them.

One raven was of particular interest to our family. Most people do not know that ravens have the physical capacity to talk in the same way a parrot talks. This bird had quite a religious vocabulary due to its rescue as an infant in the Big Sur area of the California Coast by an enclave of nuns. One of the sisters who had heard about our park showed up one day with an unusual request of me. She was leaving shortly to write a book at Oxford University in England and requested that I watch her bird until her return. When I inquired when that might be, she hesitated and explained "several years". After I explained my stance on returning all wild birds that I rehabilitated back into the natural world-if at all possible, she decided against leaving her raven with me. However, several weeks later she showed up with her raven and said she had a change of heart, and she knew her raven deserved a chance to be free. We made a temporary place for her in one of our barn out- buildings and began our interface.

The first obstacle that had to be overcome was my gender. Our newest family addition had been raised by women and was not comfortable around men. After discovering the going would be slow due to this fact my lovely wife volunteered to help. Raven loved Carol and we all became fast friends over several months of gentle care. We could literally take Raven for walks with the family and she would fly above us only to land on Carol's shoulder when we called her down. My hope had been that she would begin to interface with other wild ravens and that is what began to happen. Then on one of our walks, after several months, she glided effortlessly toward a flock of ravens, tipped her wings to us, as if to say thanks for your help, and became part of the natural world once again. When she disappeared over our ridge line we each shared tears of joy for our temporary family member.

Another fond animal nation memory is that of a magnificent full bodied mountain lion drinking from the edge of our lake. My oldest son and I were fishing from our raft at the time. I had been inspired in my early years as a naturalist by most everything author Ed Abbey had written, including a wonderful short story about looking into the eyes of a mountain lion. He had explained that experience as being one of his most powerful in the wild. I felt the same way as I looked at the huge cat with nervous anticipation. That magnificent creature was around four foot long with a tail that must have stretched another three feet. It was a tan straw color and perhaps 200 pounds of raw muscle. My heart rate increased as we peered at each other. It took a short drink from the edge of our pond and was gone like a ghost. I saw its approximately three inch wide paw prints for a week throughout my park. That was the last sign of a big cat during my years there. Scientists have verified that they can cover one hundred miles in a day. Its cry in the wild made the hair stand up on the back of my neck. I will always be especially grateful for that experience.

Moderate temperatures throughout our years in that wilderness created a lasting relationship to the water that dissected the valley via our river and lakes. Our sun bleached raft made from recycled wood and barrels of air became a constant connection to the water and to the Huckleberry Finn in each of us. Morning or evening excursions, with light fishing tackle, brought us hours of enjoyment while fishing for blue gill and bass. You literally could not keep them off of your line which is important when you are trying to entertain children. I have fond memories of my youngest son, in a front pack on my chest, my middle son, in the backpack over my shoulders, and my oldest son, hand in mine or his mothers, poling around that cattail framed body of water.

By the river we would cavort in pools large enough for the kids to swim. The largest of these was suitable for the adults to submerge into the refreshing stream to enjoy a baptism perfect to relieve summer temperatures as high as 115 degrees. We were surrounded by lizard like resting places on huge granite boulders that were displayed like a child's giant marbles along its edges. Perch or planted trout could on occasion be seen in certain eddies which would fall to lower elevations downriver. Our golden retrievers hunted the crayfish in the same manner as our heron population. Holding their heads absolutely still and then darting underneath the waters to claim their prizes, they would proudly display their fishing prowess to the family and then enjoy the fruits of their labor.

I often meandered down to the edge of our river or lakes at night to hear the songs of the frogs and other wild things. On one pitch black moonless night I could hear animals running towards me by our first lake. I knew there was more than one by the sounds being made. I could not tell how big they were. It was literally as black out as the light was in a stone-people-lodge. As they came nearer, I must have jumped as high as a kid on a trampoline. The bobcats veered away at the last moment. I am certain they were probably as startled as I was by their presence. They were approximately two and a half feet tall with tan colored bodies. I estimated they were perhaps thirty pounds in weight, with short tails and pointed ears. My heart didn't slow down until I made it back to our house to explain the entire scene to my wife who couldn't stop laughing.

I spent many quiet moments of meditation with my Chanunpa along its banks. One of my favorite places to pray with it was atop a granite platform that became known to our family as "turtle rock". It was there I made several breakthroughs on my transformational path of becoming what Black Elk called a "real human being". Grandfather and Red Buffalo discussed the telepathy that existed between human beings and all life on many occasions with me. They believed it to be a remnant of how things were in the first age on the planet when oral histories talked about direct communication amongst all forms of life in the animal, vegetable, and mineral kingdoms. Moreover, they said that people these days were generally going too fast in their lives to take time to listen to what the other life forms had to say. They explained that the telepathy was like an electrical current that could be approached with the proper focus and intent. "You must nurture the respect you have for all beings as that is essential to connect to any of the other life forms we share the Earth Mother with," Black Elk explained.

"No selfish thoughts can be present for your encounter to be effective," Red Buffalo added. "These nations will help you collect your powers. They all have intelligence." A great blue heron stunned me with the power and clarity of this kind of message. I find it fascinating that the great blue heron is often utilized by indigenous peoples as a symbol for the Sacred Way. After strolling down our trail to "turtle rock" with my Chanunpa to say my prayers one late afternoon, I had begun my pipe filling song to fill my Chanunpa when a great regal looking bird flew in directly over my head. As I sang my song I lost sight of it briefly in the horizon line of the willow, alder, sycamore, and oak trees along the valley floor. As I began to smoke my Chanunpa, I remember offering my thanks for all the gifts my family and I had received from Great Spirit. The great blue heron again caught my eye, as it then circled in the clear ultramarine blue sky. It then gracefully landed on another granite boulder at the level of the water below my perch. I believe it was only twenty feet away. It looked to me to be an adult with a height over four feet and a wing span I guessed at around six feet. Its wing color was the typical two tones of gray fringed by black. It looked grayish blue overall with a black plume extending from the back of its head as if it had hair that was permanently blowing in the breeze. It displayed a distinctly heavy pointed yellow bill. I remained perfectly still and remember thinking that the wise bird had not seen me. It stood tall, neck extended, and then it became motionless for several minutes. As if in slow motion, it turned its head directly at me until one eye locked on me as if it were a State fair hypnotist. We stayed that way for what I believe to be somewhere in the neighborhood of an hour. Neither of us moved.

Somewhere out of the ethers its thoughts were directed to me. I held my Chanunpa in front of my body with stem pointed toward it. Then it communicated to me, "I appreciate all the work that you have accomplished during your teachings in my environment." The air rustled between us. A shiver ran through me when it began to communicate again. After a long pause it noted, "There are very few who can still communicate in the old way." Then the shocking news was delivered to me, "You will need to prepare your family for a major change. You will be moving to another home." I went numb for several minutes as I thought of leaving my beloved sanctuary that I had spent many years nurturing. After several moments of silence it lifted off from the rock. Its eye was still piercing me as it soared around the next bend of the river beyond my view. It disappeared into the canopy of California Sycamore and dense willow.

That regal bird was indeed a prophet. I had been promoted and transferred. Its words echoed in my mind as I pondered the thought of leaving the place where I was learning so much. As it turned out the move that we made several months later taught me many extremely important lessons. One of those was that access to the hidden reality of nature could be achieved anywhere in the universe. I said my tearful goodbyes to my animal, vegetable, and mineral friends at Wilderness Gardens, where much of my progress on my own "Sacred Way" had begun.

I would soon be sent to the busiest park in our system. It would seem like living in a huge city after my years of isolation.

CHAPTER 11
HEALING AND HELP

I utilized over two hundred stone-people-lodges to further my education and jump-start the next phase of my development as a sacred man. Black Elk and Red Buffalo agreed I needed to fine tune my focus to bring back information from the spiritual realms that a wichasa wakan is able to access. They explained that the ability to move between the worlds with clarity was an acquired skill of an experienced practitioner. I explained to them that although I had been able to accomplish what they referred to on many occasions, I did not really know how it had occurred. They each mentioned I needed to be patient.

The spirits direct a wichasa wakan to practice what he or she has learned in a specific way. No two shamans utilize their helpers in exactly the same manner nor do they have the same helpers or "spiritual allies". Over the course of my direct training, I witnessed my teachers receive sacred instructions from these energies in many of the ceremonies that I took part in. This information came from a knowledge base that science would consider to be unexplainable.

Sometimes that knowledge could come in the form of a song to use when facilitating a healing or curing. Or they might be given specific instructions on how to help someone and be guided to pass along that information immediately. Each of my mentors gave credit for a successful ceremony to the higher powers. "Sometimes a healer has to go to extraordinary lengths to achieve the results that are sought. An icshe wichasa has to have faith that the curing they facilitate will become reality." In one of our teaching sessions on the subject, Grandfather related he had to go to Fitzsimmons Army Medical Hospital in Denver, Colorado, to help a little boy who not long after a normal birth had developed symptoms of not being able to take in nourishment nor control his own muscles to sit-up or walk. Consequently at five years of age the child was the size of a baby. After getting permission from the Hospital Board to perform a healing ceremony in the child's room at the hospital, the room was prepared in the same way as a house ceremony. All reflective surfaces were covered and the lights were turned off to create the black light of deep space. A doctor and a nurse were on hand to share the experience. What was seen by everyone in the room, after the singing of the sacred songs, was a light in the form of a man. Black Elk said this spirit man talked to him and told him that a spider web existed on one of the two main nerves in the brain that connects to the child's body. Grandfather was told he needed to get help from the *iktomi*, "spider nation". He said a red spider responded to his request to take the web from the child. Almost immediately the child could make new sounds and when the spirit helper told Black Elk that the child would be able to eat and drink on his own for the first time, he did so. "I sang an honoring song, the four winds song, and the two calling songs. The spirit man said the child's muscles would grow normally-and they did. The prayer-robes, prayer-ties, and food were missing at the end of that sacred time. Grandson, what we call physical reality seems to morph in unusual ways when these practices are being performed in the correct manner."

Black Elk's and Red Buffalo's healing efforts sometimes involved the acquisition of a sacred plant or herb to help in the healing of a sickness.

On certain occasions they might have the plant in their possession in their shaman's suitcase. Other times they were advised by Spirit where to find the plant and how to utilize its curing capabilities. On other occasions physical specimens of plants showed up out of the ethers in front of people who had asked for help or the part of the plant needed was left on the altar during a ceremony. In this manner a stone could appear inside the lodge of a shaman to be utilized in a certain way to help bring about the results needed. Sometimes the *Wakinyan,* "thunder-beings" would reveal their presence by creating tiny lightning's within the confines of the lodges. I witnessed these dance around the stones or a patient on numerous occasions. Sometimes animal shapes were seen inside the ceremonies and other times unique shapes of colored lights were visible. On many occasions bird sounds could be heard or a feather might manifest to be utilized in the curing. When help manifested in physical form everyone connected to the ceremony was extremely grateful.

Space, time, matter, and energy seemed to be manipulated during a ceremony. Grandfather spoke to me about helping authorities on one occasion to find out about a murder. On another occasion he helped find the whereabouts of a downed airplane. Regarding other matters certain practitioners were able to accomplish the help needed with an unusual shift in their focus.

Other Lakota rituals were utilized to bring about healings and curing as well. Red Buffalo shared with me the story of a *hanbleycha*, the Lakota form of "vision quest", facilitated by Black Elk, in which the spirits cured him of a cancer his western physicians had diagnosed. Black Elk had put Red Buffalo on the vision quest hill for four days and nights with no food or water near his Yankton home to ask Spirit for help. A complete cure was facilitated soon afterwards. Red Buffalo explained to me, "Doubt is a great destroyer of success for this sacred medicine way." He went on to say that his healing had solidified his own belief system. In his ceremonies and those of Black Elk's they usually asked that all shadows of doubt be put away so the powers could do their work.

Undoubtedly, the most important moment of my early training came when my middle son was diagnosed as legally blind in one eye. We were shocked to learn during a check-up with our pediatrician that he was 20x400, which is considered legally blind in one eye. His optic nerve was diagnosed as being under developed and the cause of his defect. We were told that there was no cure. Follow-up eye patching was recommended.

After discussing the matter, my wife and I asked for help from Red Buffalo on his already planned visit to our park. I presented my Chanunpa to him after I filled it as I had been taught. I passed it to him four times in the traditional manner. As I passed it the fourth time, I asked for a curing for my sons damaged eye. He accepted my Chanunpa. If he could not help he would have rejected my pipe. After several minutes of stark silence, his spiritual allies advised him that we could accomplish the work in a stone-people-lodge ceremony. He went on to explain that my young son would not have to be part of the lodge environment. Red Buffalo would sing the sacred songs and pour the water the evening we planned the healing ceremony. As the fireman I would build the fire and pray over each stone that we brought in. I would also help with the singing and prayers. We smoked my Chanunpa and our plan was put in motion.

On the evening of the healing ritual Red Buffalo cautioned me that he might need to leave his physical body to find out something related to the healing process during our ceremony. He said it was very dangerous to be out of his body if people "disturbed his physical robe", in what looked like a man sleeping to the casual observer. I assured him I would continue my prayers until he came back. People unfamiliar with these practices would think the shaman had passed away and Red Buffalo explained to me that in the past a wichasa wakan had almost died because someone had interfered. He emphasized how serious this path could become.

I set up the sacred fire as per instructions from the spirits and meditated on the healing while waiting for the stones to heat up. I hung 405 prayer ties in six colors for the spiritual help that would enter that stone-people-lodge at Red Buffalo's request. A red sprit-robe was hung in the North for help from the buffalo nation. A yellow sprit-robe was hung in the East for help from the elk and deer nations. A white spirit-robe was hung in the South for help from all the other nations. A black spirit-robe was hung in the West for help from the thunder beings. A blue spirit-robe and a green spirit-robe were hung between the red and black robes for help from the Earth Mother herself and all that exists above the earth, *Wakan Tanka*. The intent was set. Red Buffalo also tied brown patterned prayer ties for help from the iktomi nation. He explained that spider medicine helpers were experts when it came to repairing nerves in the human body.

I helped him with the songs throughout each segment of our stone-people-lodge ceremony. I never saw him leave his body. He sang with me throughout our sacred time. During the second segment of the ceremony I witnessed brilliant white lights floating inside of the stone-people-lodge after the songs and prayers were completed. They appeared as orbs of light about the size of softballs just like the first lodge I ever attended with him. The temperature seemed to rise several degrees upon their arrival.

When it came time for me to pray I felt the sensation of feathers all over my face, softly blessing me. My focus intensified with the heat in the third segment of our ceremony. I could make out the silhouette of a large red shape that looked to be that of a bird flying in the dark expanse of the interior space during this spirit filled time. I could hear the flapping of its wings and knew the moment it entered the structure because I heard the sound above me against the roof of the lodge.

The heat grew so intense it drove me to the floor of the enclosure during the fourth and last segment of the curing. I felt like candle wax that had melted from an intense flame. The crescendo of heat subsided as we opened the blanket flap. We were too drained to move at first. We just sprawled out flat against the earth in the pool of moisture that existed within that stone-people-lodge circle. The mud on the floor of the lodge never felt better. We ended the ceremony by smoking our Chanunpas and sharing the sacred food. We always brought water, corn, berries, and meat to honor the Spirits that helped. We walked slowly back to my house without saying a word.

Next morning he asked to talk to me privately.

He revealed to me these words, "The Spirits say that your son's eye will improve in a dramatic manner. They say his vision will never be perfect in that eye but they have improved his sight to where it will be quite functional." My son achieved 20x40 vision in that eye after the healing that took place. His vision remains strong.

"Iktomi helpers are some of the most powerful healing spirits," Red Buffalo stated. "You have been given a powerful gift, and so has your son."

This ceremony and many others created my special perspective about the "sacred mystery powers". It seemed obvious to me that science had overlooked a sacred reality hidden in the culture of a people that were overrun centuries before. Quantum physics was a subject I was being taught by the Spirits themselves.

CHAPTER 12
LAKOTA VISION QUEST-HANBLEYCHA

Black Elk, and Red Buffalo, encouraged me to utilize any opportunity to be with *Wakan Tanka*, "Great Spirit", in the wilds of the natural world. They said this was where a Lakota wichasa wakan gained many of their powers.

Black Elk encouraged me further knowing my park schedule and family responsibilities, "Grandson, even if you only are able to stay several hours, or several days, the Spirits will honor your good intentions". He stated that initially he had been taught that four days and nights was essential.

However, over time his spirit helpers had divulged otherwise. He said he now counted twelve hour stretches of time as one day.

"Instruction from Spirit is like lightning. It doesn't strike if there is no receiver. You must stay aware at all times during your meditation and prayers with nature. To really understand it you have to listen to your heart and mind. You must stand before Great Spirit in isolation. It might sound simple but sometimes it can be really tough. When you are there you will have to go inside the power where there is no fear and no pain. It can be an incredibly beautiful experience. Wisdom, knowledge, power, and love can be found there," Grandfather explained.

Black Elk's instructions were very clear in my mind as I worked my way through the switched back trail system in the thick chaparral elfin forest moving toward the ridge line on my first hanbleycha. I had cut a trail to some ancient pictographs in the area above my park using deer paths about a month before.

"The first part of our word for hanbleycha means to fast, or attain a vision. The second part of the word means to intensely pray. To break that word down even further 'han' means night and 'ble' means quiet place," Black Elk added.

Red Buffalo encouraged me further, "Go up on your mountain-or anywhere in the arms of the Earth Mother. Use your intent to make a deep connection to Spirit. We do not need to be there with you. In our tradition we ingest no food or water during this sacred time. The spirits will help you decide how long you remain on the hill."

To begin a traditional hanbleycha a person usually asks the help of a sacred man. They assist by performing a purification stone-people-lodge ritual prior to the individual being brought to a mountain site or in their family vision pit site to fast and pray for a vision. A seasoned wichasa wakan feels what the vision quester feels during their isolation with spirit. They literally are already aware of what the vision quester has experienced prior to their return. After a set amount of time they go back up the mountain to retrieve the vision quester and usually help them to understand what has taken place while performing another stone-people-lodge. The Chanunpa is smoked to end the sacred rite.

I was told I should accomplish my hanbleycha's on my own in a stone-people-lodge ceremony my mentors and I completed. This allowed me the freedom to accomplish this part of my training without them.

After a stone-people-lodge in which I heated up just seven stones and completed two doors of prayers I prepared for my walk and vision quest. As I strode up the roughed out trail in my moccasins wearing only a pair of loose gym shorts, I carried my medicine bundle in a small pack on my back. An hour later I got to my site and covered the ground with sage to form my "nest" as Grandfather called it. I then created an altar area for my Chanunpa and other medicine articles. I strung my prayer ties on the four sticks I had placed in the four directions and hung my eagle feather on a stick propped up by rocks as I had been instructed. I had chosen that site because of the ancient pictographs on adjacent boulders nearby where others had called in their helpers. They were located in an isolated part of that mountain that would afford me a view of the valley below with no interruptions. I thought of Black Elk and Red Buffalo as they had performed that ancient rite many times over many years of practice.

My prayer-ties and spirit-robes created a sacred rectangular space on my natural clay porch amidst a plethora of several different varieties of sage, ceanothus, wild buckwheat, and other elfin forest scrub. Red Buffalo had reminded me that while I was up there I would become the altar. Grandfather had explained that real spirits would wear the cloth of my robes.

The cerulean colors of the sky seemed to intensify as the day wore on. The grays and greens of the chaparral were spectacular. I could hear the sounds of red-tailed and red-shouldered hawks as they rode the thermals of the slight breeze above the canyon where I knew my family was wondering about me. I heard and saw meadowlarks, poorwills, ravens, towhees, finches, sparrows, wrens, flycatchers, red-winged blackbirds, and others. I prayed, and sang, and observed it all. My focus sharpened.

My first night was spent in the same manner, however, the temperature was much more pleasant and the stars were a magnificent tunnel of lights and twinkling's. My hunger was not what hit me hard. It was my intense thirst. Black Elk had informed me that on several of his hanbleycha's putting some sage in his mouth had soothed his dry brittle mouth and lips. The sage began to do the same for me. I was greatly relieved when the sun went down on my second day on the hill. The night air was soothing as a droplet of sweat fell to the ground before me. My throat felt like sandpaper. The stars in the sky above me looked close enough to touch. I had held my Chanunpa for so long my hands and arms were cramping. It cooled down further and the stars again took over my attention as if they were blinking some sort of cosmic Morse code.

Then it happened out of the West. A huge form perhaps four feet high by five feet long approached me. I was extremely nervous. Fear gripped my solar plexus. I realized I was not dreaming. I remembered in that next instant the coaching I had received. "Stay focused and do not be afraid", were Red Buffalo's words. I resisted my desire to get up and run. I really wanted to run. As it walked slowly towards me I could see it was clearly the shape of a wolf. A very large black spirit wolf whose form and shape I could literally see through. I held my Chanunpa directly in front of me and thanked it for coming. I was surrounded by the thickness of the dark of the night. I do not know how long it remained motionless watching me. Then I received these words from that wolf. "Thank you for your prayers. The Chanunpa is sacred. Always honor your Sacred Way." It then wandered off into the brush before me. I stayed ready for any other appearances that night, but there were none.

When the sun began to rise next morning it was time to come down from my mountain perch. I was both exhausted and excited. I felt loneliness like I had never experienced before.

On my way down that mountain I took a wrong turn through some thick brush and ended up having to create a new path through the chaparral thickets to make it back. I was scratched up and bleeding when I finally hit a familiar part of the trail. I smiled through it all as I had been visited by a spirit helper that would return to help me in my own medicine work. I connected to the wolf nation on that very first hanbleycha and the solitary manner in which a wolf goes about his business is very comfortable for me.

While backpacking in Alaska, several years later, I was traveling along a ridge line trail above an expanse of river. It sat perhaps only a hundred yards below me. From this position I had the great fortune to see an unusual struggle not many have seen in the wild. There before me was a regal looking moose, perhaps six feet high, weighing somewhere in the vicinity of one thousand pounds. This brown creature with large overhanging snout and massive antlers was in combat with another mammal that was initially hidden by the sheer size of the moose, whose head was pushed forward as it strained to keep the other animal away from its legs. When the smaller animal moved to get a better angle on his food source I realized I was looking at a gray wolf approximately three and half feet tall, perhaps four feet long, weighing somewhere in the vicinity of one hundred and fifty pounds. Its tail must have measured an additional foot to a foot and a half in length. The dark gray creature moved back and forth attacking the legs of the moose for over an hour. When finally the moose succumbed to the forays its limp body floated down stream where I noticed for the first time the wolf pack waiting at the end of several switch-backs in the river. Those eight family members dragged the moose ashore as I followed the alpha wolf around the turns of the oxbows in the river, through my binoculars, to where he joined in the feast.

Again the realization struck me that we are indeed all related on the great Circle of Life.

CHAPTER 13
LOOKING AT THE SUN THEY DANCE

I tried to focus my eyes in the now dimming twilight toward the open ground in front of us. Several hundred yards of brush covered meadow expanded before us into the gloaming twilight. We had disappeared into the shadows behind a grouping of cottonwood trees along the Missouri River near the Yankton Indian Reservation. Red Buffalo was in quiet meditation by my side.

The deer appeared out of the shadows no more than fifty yards away. As he moved slowly towards our position I could make out a modest antler crown of perhaps four spikes. He presented himself like royalty at a coronation. He stopped motionless for a split second and turned his head until his gaze rested in our direction. He seemed to have waited for the shot that Red Buffalo had just taken. We had prayed the evening before in a stone-people-lodge for such an occurrence to take place.

Red Buffalo and I prayed over that deer for several minutes in the diminishing light. We each gave thanks to the spirit of the deer and the nourishment he would provide for the Sun Dance feast. We then loaded him into his pickup for our ride back to his home. His family and supporters would have meat to eat before and after the Sun Dance.

"It will be an opportunity for you to meet the rest of my family and friends, and experience another Sun Dance as part of your training," Red Buffalo serenely stated to me in a telephone conversation prior to the ritual. He knew I had been able to break away from my job for several short stints at Black Elk's Sun Dances outside of Ashland, Oregon. My very busy park's summer schedule had never allowed me to experience a full dance from preparation to completion and give away. He seemed certain I would be there, even though at the time we spoke I had no idea where I would get the money for the trip. Nor did I know if I could get the time off from my work. As spiritual serendipity played out, a birthday present from my sister Karen and some well orchestrated scheduling at my park allowed for the teaching. My mother-in-law helped Carol cover my duties with my family.

"The Sun Dance shows us the interdependence and interconnectedness of all things. It extends the meaning of 'to all my relations' to mean we are all of one blood," Red Buffalo declared. He had encouraged me to sing and pray at his drum. He knew I had not received a vision to be in the circle as a dancer.

Red Buffalo had originally lived on the Cheyenne Indian Reservation where he had been a policeman until relocating his family to the Yankton Reservation where he had become a practicing wicasa wakan after his own spiritual awakening. After he picked me up at the airport I purchased as many supplies for the Red Buffalo family as my budget allowed. Upon my arrival at his property, I set up my dome tent on a knoll about 100 yards from their simple weathered wood-sided house. His land became a modified campground each year for this sacred ceremony when tipis and tents could be seen from many of its corners. Several weeks before the dance his well water pump had given out and there was not money enough to purchase a replacement. We made several trips to haul water for the supporters in attendance which gave us plenty of time to talk privately.

"To gaze at the sun while dancing and to be gazed at by the sun while dancing can be a life changing experience," he stated with clarity.

"The word 'ceremony' means 'in a circle'. Now I am giving back to Great Spirit by sponsoring this Sun Dance."

"The dance itself should be held during the full moon when the berries ripen. New moon to new moon-June to July is sometimes utilized. Or it should take place during the days when the cherries blacken which is middle of July to middle of August. Grandfather Nicholas Black Elk said it should always be held during a full moon because the waxing and waning reminds us of our wisdom and ignorance. The full moon reminds us that our knowledge of the eternal Light of Great Spirit is best understood when the moon is rising at the same time the sun is setting. The Sun Dance is a picture of our relationship to that which is being honored, *Takuskanskan*, 'that which causes all things to move in the universe'. Through our Chanunpa, our 'Tree of Life', we see with understanding. As intercessor, I will be an instrument of the power working in that sacred circle." He related that there were to be around sixteen dancers at this year's ritual. However, there might be nearly a hundred supporters over the four days of the actual dance.

I was there to pray at Red Buffalo's Sun Dance drum and support him and his family as much as possible. Grandmother Spotted Eagle, before she passed over, and Yellow Cloud, another Black Elk family member and noted ceremonial singer, were responsible for much of my progress in this area.

"The ceremonial singers are an important part of the Sun Dance and your prayers are essential. You will feel the heart of the dance from this position," he instructed very seriously.

Prior to the dance, friends from his community and others visiting from out of town were enlisted to build the shade arbor for those in attendance who would not be dancing. We spent three days building two concentric circles of forked poles approximately twenty eight paces from the center where the Sun Dance tree would be located. The poles were joined on two sides by saplings and boughs of leafy vegetation. These are then attached to the top to form the shade arbor. Because this vegetation is highly sought after we had to drive quite a distance to find the materials we needed along the Missouri River.

We began at dawn the following day after Red Buffalos mother spoke to the crowd over a microphone installed for this four day period of the full moon. The ceremony began with the selection of a place where the hole would be dug for the sacred tree. "On the first day a worthy man is selected to find an appropriate cottonwood tree. We utilize a tree where its forks are at a height above where the ropes will be tied. It is believed that the power of the sun and star knowledge rests there until the dancers need it. When the tree is erected the fork sits on the North and South axis. It points to the two ends of the Milky Way. We call that the spirit trail."

Red Buffalo selected one of his local friends to dig the hole for the sacred tree. He removed dirt from the hole to create the altar to the West where a buffalo robe was placed. On the fourth day of this dance this altar was where the piercing took place.

"We give a little of our own blood to thank creator for all the blessings we have received. We are humble. We know that is all that we as humans really have to give the Creator." Sixty four paces to the East was where the sacred tipi was placed. This structure was where the Sun Dancers would receive their instruction and where they would sleep and rest while not in the dance circle. When this tipi is erected those that are dancing begin their fasts. This tipi is considered lela wakan. We faced the door to the West when we erected it and then lined its floor with sage we had picked on a hike together earlier in the week. We placed an altar on the West side with a buffalo skull stuffed with sage.

A stone-people-lodge structure with a West facing door was already in place in the North and offerings of tobacco were attached to the stakes that formed the path to the sun. "The dancers may purify in the stone-people- lodge as much as four times a day until the day of the dance," he said. "And if you can help with those sacred fires as a helper and singer you will be allowed to join the dancers inside those purification ceremonies." He said the words with a little grin on his face, knowing how much I had grown to appreciate the heat.

"Spirit will direct the man I have assigned to choose the tree appropriate for the ritual. I want you to be part of the party that goes out to harvest the tree." Perhaps a dozen friends and supporters made up the tree acquisition group. We sang songs with great reverence after we arrived at its base. We then asked it for its help at the Sun Dance in silent prayers. Red Buffalo then offered his Chanunpa to the powers of the four directions. He pointed it at the tree four times.

A young girl is always chosen to make the first axe blow after which in a clockwise fashion several men cut the tree until it is almost ready to fall. Then another young girl who has not yet begun her moon time is asked to make the final cut. The tree was felled to the South and it was trimmed until only the forked branches were exposed. We then loaded it into a long-bed pickup truck and brought it back to camp. We stopped four times along our way to sing the appropriate songs and those involved in the cutting were asked to purify themselves in a stone-people-lodge.

At the directed time Red Buffalo asked several of us to raise the pole. We placed the butt end in the hole where the sacred food had been placed. Spiritual symbols were placed in the tree. A sacred song was sung and dirt was then packed around it. "During the first three days those who have pledged to sacrifice themselves meet with me to tell me their dream. 'To dance gazing at the sun', *wi wayang wacipi*. 'To pierce with wooden or bone skewers, inserted into the chest above the breasts, that are attached to rawhide ropes about halfway up the tree', *wicapalokapi*. 'To hang suspended and pierced between four posts', *okaske wacipi*. Or 'to be pierced above the shoulder blades and drag buffalo skulls around the dance area', *ptepap yusichanpi*. In the last three forms, the dancers sacrifice themselves until the flesh has torn or a supporter expedites their release if their suffering is long."

Those who took part in the dance wore red kilts made of cotton cloth or hide. Some wore moccasins and others were bare footed. Eagle bone whistles hung around most of the dancers necks by cords with eagle plumes attached. The dancers followed Red Buffalo who carried a painted buffalo skull along the south side of their sacred tipi. They circled the sacred space of the Sun Dance four times sun-wise. They then entered the sacred grounds. Wreaths of sage were displayed on their heads. Anklets and wristlets of sage helped create the sacred human. As we sang the opening song on the drum, the Sun Dance started and they moved toe-heel, toe-heel, in a line, blowing on their eagle whistles in time with our drum. During this time they faced each of the four directions.

After a time the singers at the drum were offered a Chanunpa by two participants selected by Red Buffalo. They danced up to our drum, holding their Chanunpas and after four offerings the lead singer accepted the pipes and we smoked them while all the dancers rested.

Red Buffalo started the dance again and it went on at intervals throughout that day. This went on each of the three days prior to the last. I became mesmerized by the beat of the drum. At the end of each day the singers were invited to participate with the Sun Dancers in their purification ceremonies inside the stone-people-lodge. I was humbled by their courage, strength, and endurance. I could see some were having a more difficult time than others. A mixture of sage tea was passed out as medicine within the circle of those participants. It is common knowledge amongst the dancers that within the Sun Dance Circle many of the miraculous phenomenon of this Sacred Way may possibly occur. There were several stories of such healings inside our purification lodges.

On the fourth day of Red Buffalo's Sun Dance his assistant made the proper incisions with surgical tools for each dancer who had made the decision to pierce. They were taken one by one to the place prepared for this activity within the circle. Some displayed more of their pain than others. Their skewers were placed within their incisions. These were two small cuts several inches above each breast allowed for the bone or wood to be placed just under their skin. They were then led back to their place in the circle and tied to the tree by the ropes that had been placed there before the dance. These razor tools were changed out for each dancer so as not to contaminate any blood from one to another. Most dancers began moving back and forth, between the tree and the tension of their ropes as soon as they were attached. Others were involved in long prayers at the tree. It is said the trunk of that sacred tree often feels like human skin after four days of dancing. They would eventually break free from their ropes and the tree, with a splash of blood, finishing their dance. Some struggled to break free. Two dancers chose to be pierced from the skin near their shoulder blades where their bone skewers were placed and their ropes were tied to huge buffalo skulls which they dragged very painfully around the sacred circle. They were not attached directly to the tree yet showed great bravery as the skulls stretched their skin unmercifully. These prayers of incredible intensity and courage ended with two little children being placed on the skulls allowing the ropes to be pulled free. Often times many turns around the circle meant excruciating pain for that participant.

After four days of singing and praying and taking part in numerous stone-people-lodges, I felt a power moving through my veins. Something about the movements had altered my ordinary consciousness. It seemed to connect me directly to the umbilical cord of the Earth Mother herself. She tugged at my own solar plexus. I felt her consciousness and a love-filled warmth flow through me. Gratitude filled my heart as my emotions overwhelmed me. I wept for the planet and man's relationship to her.

There was great rejoicing after the dancers ordeal was over. A feast was completed that evening followed by a giveaway the next afternoon.

One of my great lessons was learned through the generosity I saw at the family giveaway. This is considered one of the noble traits of the Earth People and often accompanies a special occasion like marriage, birth, or Sun Dance.

Red Buffalo's family gave their community beautiful crafts, blankets, and other useful items. A family that had so little in the way of material possessions showed a caring and love for others that made me quite emotional.

In that giveaway Red Buffalo's mother called me to the center of the gathering and presented me a star blanket. It was hand sewn with red and violet colored shapes that made up the star. She stated that she had made it for me "At the request of the spirits. You will need this for the work that I see in your future." I saw the wide grin on Red Buffalo's face when I held it up for all to see. What a thrill.

I could hear and feel the beat of the drum as I fell asleep exhausted that night. My voice was nearly gone. I was hoarse from four days of singing and praying. I flew back home the next afternoon. I felt I had experienced something I would cherish forever. I have taken that blanket with me on many hanbleychas. My admiration for the Red Buffalo family will always accompany me.

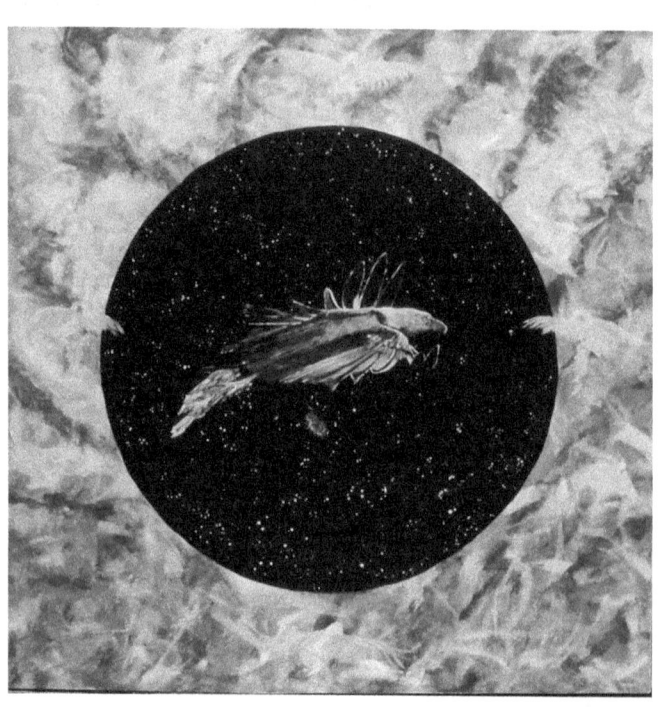

CHAPTER 14
COUNCIL WITH EAGLES

It was not the snow-covered majesty of its mountains, the crystal clarity of its lakes or rivers, the mirror-like blue reflections of its glaciers, the wild and glorious gold stories, or the million acre tracts of virgin tundra that first drew me to Alaska. It was the bald eagle population that I hoped to find in an area along the banks of the Chilkat River. The natives called it "Eagle Council Grounds". This location became the irresistible force that tugged at me in dreamtime.

Stories about bald eagles by the thousands along the Chilkat River drew me like a magnet draws iron. The eagles congregate for winter feasting on salmon there and many remain year round.

During a stone-people-lodge ceremony with Grandfather Black Elk, he said, "On your hanbleycha you will receive instructions from elders at the place of eagles," and he asked me to pray for eagle feathers for his Sun Dancers. Because of modern day protections for eagles some of the Sun Dancers had a hard time finding the feathers necessary to utilize in their ancient rite. I pondered that information for many weeks before my own guides directed me to Eagle Council Grounds in Alaska. I planned a three week trek. Two days and nights would be spent fasting and praying for a vision in one of the most impressive areas for bald eagles in the world.

As a young man I had become fascinated with tales about the gold miners of the Klondike and the recession of the 1890's. Thousands had quit their jobs and sold their homes to seek their fortune in the Alaskan wilderness. John Muir wrote eloquently about the high country grandeur of Alaska. He viewed it as a wilderness paradise. Many regarded it only as a frozen wasteland suitable for exploitation. They were only interested in the hides, gold, salmon, and oil.

My journey began with a plane ride from San Diego to Seattle. From there I ferried up the inside passage to my hanbleycha site along the Chilkat River. After completing my hanbleycha I worked my way up to the Arctic Circle via rental car. I then went South leading me into the backcountry of Denali. I finished my journey with another plane ride out of Anchorage back home. I have fond memories of backpack excursions with grizzly bears, wolves, moose, caribou, mountain goats, loons, hawks, owls, and numerous significant others.

I plotted a northern course via ferry that allowed for a savoring of the rich history and beauty of the Inside Passage in the Southeast. This waterway is made up of thousands of islands, fjords, and steep mountain coastlines. As a backpacker I was allowed to pitch my tent in the rear open space of the vessel. Stops in Prince Rupert B.C., Wrangell, Petersburg, Sitka, Juneau, and Haynes left me with a heightened sense of excitement as I neared the access point for my connection to the Chilkat. I hired a rafting company out of Haines to drop me off at the Council Grounds site. They agreed to return for me after forty-eight hours.

Because this was not the heart of winter, but instead a mild Alaskan July, I was unsure if many eagles would be at my destination. Many had circled high above the ferry, however, as if to follow my northern trail.

As we set out upstream on the Chilkat River my rafting guide instructed me that the river was low and our trip would be relatively calm. He judged the sparkling clear water to be less than twelve feet deep in many sections. He said deeper pools under bedrock ledges could be found both above us and below. I felt intense loneliness between those stretches of spruce where tundra went up the sides of mountain ridges and I missed my family terribly. Bear tracks could be seen everywhere along my route and overcoming my fear became a part of my journey. We passed miles of spruce and cottonwood trees. The forests were so thick I couldn't imagine how one could pass through those areas on terra firma, without the river itself acting like a magical doorway. Occasionally a turn in the river would reveal eagles circling overhead moving and soaring along the thermals giving me hope for a positive encounter.

Another moment of fear gripped me as my rafting guide waved good-bye and said he would return in two days as I had requested. No elders had contacted me and I wondered about Black Elk's previous statement to me at our stone-people-lodge. I experienced a feeling of disorientation that I overcame as I surveyed a flat area that would serve me well, just above the river's edge, hidden in the trees. I could see anything on the river from this vantage point. I stored my gear, a sleeping bag, and my backpack with the barest of necessities, along a ledge of rock above me. I had eaten the last of my food-a piece of jerky and washed it down with a cup of camp coffee along the way. It would have to hold me for forty-eight hours. Having no food seemed like a reasonable precaution given the tastes of the local bear population. Mosquito repellent was a must along any river that time of year.

The ancient stones along the river knew what I had come there for. My sacred time in direct communication with Great Spirit had begun. I set up my prayer-ties and spirit-robes to form the rectangular perimeter surrounding me. I next made a nest of my sage to sit on and filled my Chanunpa, to carry with me at all times within the altar that I had become a part of. I presented my eagle feather on a stick in its usual central location . The colors of my altar were presented to the powers of the four winds, and to Mother Earth and father sky and of course the eagle nation. "Your time should be focused. You will need to stay in full awareness. You are not there to sleep," were Grandfather's words.

One of my favorite quotes from N. Scott Momaday gives you a sense of a person's heightened awareness: "Once in his life a man ought to concentrate his mind upon the remembered earth. To look at it from as many angles as he can, to wonder upon it, to dwell upon it. He ought to imagine that he touches it with his hands at every season and listen to the sounds that are made upon it. He ought to view the creatures there and all the faintest motions of the wind. He ought to recollect the glare of the moon and the colors of the dawn and dusk."

I began by sitting, then standing, dancing, and praying aloud to give thanks for being there. I often pointed my Chanunpa to the heavens and asked for help for all beings. I sang the sacred songs that I had been taught to the powers of the four winds. The Milky Way appeared so close it was almost as if I could touch it during the very short nights that broke up the long light filled days of that Alaskan summer. Only a few long range views of eagles came to me at that point in my prayers.

As the sky lightened, after my second night out in the wilds of Alaska, bald eagles began to land on the level ledge above the river in front of me. I had observed many of the glorious black and white creatures fly above me. I could also see a few eagles perching in trees quite a distance away. Then out of nowhere a large brilliant black and white shape landed no more than a few yards from where my foot prints had left their impressions in my movements to the four directions. Then another, and another landed in my area; until I counted twelve eagles forming a semicircle perhaps ten yards away. Beyond those twelve I estimated another perimeter of approximately 40-50 eagles perched both high and low in the surrounding vegetation within perhaps 25 yards of what to a casual observer would have been a very unusual scene. That space and my consciousness had blended into one.

I was startled when the largest eagle in the inner grouping walked towards my area of prayerties. It then stepped inside and made eye contact with me in the same way a great blue heron had done several years before. The edges of that landscape grew in intensity and clarity as he began to speak to my mind," Thank you for your prayers of gratitude and your endurance and focus." I communicated to him then, " I am honored to be here."

Then he communicated these words, "The light throughout our universe is changing once again. Human beings have another chance to awaken after a long slumber. It is possible that all beings will have an opportunity to communicate freely again in the Fifth Age of Mankind. In the same manner as we are communicating to each other at this moment. Thoughts and dreams may merge to create a peace beyond ordinary understanding." I was very nervous but listened intently and held my Chanunpa in front of me with reverence.

The eagle communicated to me very methodically, "I have come to you in this manner to teach you the real history of your people. Would you like me to relate that story to you?" I nodded in reverence. It began a few moments later: "In the beginning Great Spirit began to form each unique shape in a translucent sphere for your world. From this realm of spirit all matter was manifested."

"Countless other entities would live as thought forms until their births into physicality, through what you call evolution. These beings were the next part of the creation matrix."

"Your people have lost the threads of memory that contain the "Great Ages" of this planet that existed prior to the one we are now in. The first ended by fire. The second ended by ice. The third ended by a great flood. Your fourth world was formed as the water receded from the surface of the earth. A Great Age of peace and joy may again be possible for humankind."

With his last statement, he bowed and stepped back to the grouping of the other eagles that had come to witness that sharing. I sat in silence and pondered what I had heard during the remaining hours of my isolation.

That afternoon my guide would arrive via raft as I cleaned my vision quest site. I rolled my prayer-ties and spirit-robes into a ball and placed them under a rock ledge as I had been taught. I then organized my gear.

The shape of an eagle faded out of my view riding high on the winds in the distance as I headed around the first bend of the Chilkat River back to my familiar world. My sons had slipped a message into my wallet with each of their pictures. They had asked me not to forget them. I missed them and their amazing mother even more after my time on my own. They were why I cared so much about helping others. I prayed for a better world for their futures.

There is really no English translation for the Lakota words lela wakan. However, I knew my experience could be described as such. In the sacred language of Sanskrit a similar word 'lila' means "cosmic play". In the Aboriginal world 'lila' means "ancestral dream". The eagle nation had become a part of who I was as a shaman.

*Please note that the Fifth World is discussed by the eagle in reference to the next "Great Age" on our planet. Many elders believe we are now in the process of moving from the Fourth World and many indigenous societies believe our recent galactic alignment marks the beginning of this transformation.

CHAPTER 15
STONE DREAMERS-YUWIPI

Black Elk and Red Buffalo explained that a *yuwipi* ceremony was one of the oldest Lakota ceremonies. "*Tunka* means stone and is our oldest name for Great Spirit. It is a ceremony that utilizes the 'power of lightning', the 'power of the buffalo', the 'power of the eagle', and the 'power of the deer'. Through dreams coming from the stones a yuwipi wichasa is able to heal or find someone, find something, or find the cause of a sickness. Sometimes they can find a piece of the future," Grandfather explained. "It is a sacred stone rite, and we have taught you that stones carry many mysterious powers. The red hot stones that you pull from the sacred fire in our purification ceremonies contain that spiritual power. A yuwipi wichasa has great courage. A 'wichasa wakan' can acquire the tying up altar on a hanbleycha to become a yuwipi man."

"How does that take place Grandfather?" I interjected. "Another yuwipi man would tie the aspiring yuwipi wichasa while he was up on the mountain completing his hanbleycha. The spirits would untie him if he was supposed to carry that specific altar. This person would become a specialist within the ranks of the sacred men," he seriously stated.

Neither Black Elk nor Red Buffalo ever "tied up" in their own healing work during our teaching time together. Red Buffalo explained in a somber tone, "During a yuwipi ceremony the yuwipi wichasa is tied with a rawhide thong by his helpers. First they tie his hands and fingers behind his back. Then they cover him with his star blanket and tie him right around his neck down to his body. This is done with seven knots and is secured very tightly to help him concentrate. He is laid face down on the floor within his altar of prayer ties on a bed of sage. In the blanket the shaman is like a butterfly in a cocoon."

My mind raced back to my own childhood when I had picked up special stones off the ground and squirreled them away in my bedroom. I was usually on the lookout in whatever I did for my collection of rocks. My cousin's neighbor who ran heavy equipment for a living used to let us rummage through his "extra stones" to keep what we liked. I still carry a few special stones from those early days and now utilize them on my own altar. One has the shape of an orca whale on its flat face. Another has the ocean with waves crashing and lightning flashing above that on its flat side.

"Most human beings have forgotten the relationship we have to all life-especially stones,"

Grandfather reminded me. "In the First Great Age of Mankind we were not conceited about such relationships. Stones have many abilities. Crystals are just one of the many stone families that carry great power. Most people now days are too skeptical to believe in the power and healing qualities of stones. A wichasa wakan needs to be faithful to the stones he utilizes on his altar. If they are not cared for properly a stone might disappear. Often that person will think they have misplaced the stone or think the stone was taken by someone when in point of truth it has traveled elsewhere. This action is called *Takuskanskan*. It is "a sacred force that causes movement of all things in our universe."

"To prepare for a yuwipi ceremony anything reflective in the room is covered with blankets or thick black plastic. The ceremony is performed in the pitch darkness of whatever space is chosen. This usually happens in the room of a participant's house. After the yuwipi wichasa is placed within his altar of sprit-robes and prayer-ties, he is tied up and the lights are turned off. He is praying to the powers of the four winds within his star blanket. Sometimes they leave their bodies to spirit travel to accomplish whatever the ceremony is about. Other times they ask their spirit helpers for assistance. After the fourth song of the 16 that are sung they begin to interpret what the spirits are saying to them.

Because Black Elk and Red Buffalo thought it would be important for my spiritual education, I attended a few of these ceremonies as a supporter. In the yuwipi ceremonies I attended there appeared to be small lights flying around the room, perhaps three to four inches across, flickering in the darkness. I was blessed each time by the touching of my head by the gourd rattle that appeared to fly around the room sometimes as high as the ceiling. Each yuwipi wichasa told me he considered this touching with the rattle a gift of power from Spirit. It is said the spirits pick-up the rattles and I heard them in front of me and also behind me. Each ceremony ended with the yuwipi man apparently being untied by the spirits associated with his altar after all the lights were turned on. His Chanunpa is then shared around the room. The yuwipi wichasa then interprets what he was told by the spirits. It is an impressive and fascinating display of the ancient powers of this sacred way.

"The yuwipi ceremony is an ancient ritual. *Yuwi* is translated as to "tie up". A yuwipi man will be untied by the spirits if he has been successful with his work . Special yuwipi songs are sung at these ceremonies to solidify our intentions and bring help from the spirits who come and untie the yuwipi man," Red Buffalo explained to me.

"Sometimes the 'sacred mystery powers' are revealed in other ways; including disappearances and reappearances of the man that is tied. At one ceremony I participated in, the spirits moved two people to another room within the house where the ceremony was taking place because they had expressed doubts about its success. Those people were very surprised when the lights went on to find themselves not by the altar where they had begun their participation," Grandfather added with a chuckle.

On another occasion Black Elk related to me that a yuwipi man had not done exactly what the spirits had advised him to do and they had found him over a mile down a road outside the house where the ceremony took place. He was still tied up.

CHAPTER 16
HOUSE CEREMONY

Black Elk and Red Buffalo utilized a variation of the form of healing ceremony that went on during a yuwipi, when a stone-people-lodge was not available or a patient could not physically crawl into a lodge. They referred to it as an *altar ceremony* or *house ceremony*. They utilized their healing skills in this manner when their spiritual guides instructed them it was the proper manner to help someone. All of the preparation was similar to a yuwipi, however, no tying up procedures were followed.

These ceremonies were often accomplished in a room of the patient's house, a friend's house, or even a hospital room. The space selected needed to be large enough to hold the shaman, singers, and any friendly supporters the patient wanted at the gathering. The supporters usually took their places against a wall away from the patient and shaman in the center of the action. In choosing those supporters Black Elk stated, "A person taking part in the ceremony, even a supporter, was required to carry only positive thoughts about the help requested. Any negative thoughts could have adverse effects on the outcome."

As in the yuwipi, all reflective surfaces were covered, and the lights were turned off, to create the pitch black of deep space. I witnessed on more than one occasion a reflective surface not covered would be discovered broken after the lights were turned on. Each of my mentors altars contained spirit-robes displayed on thin sticks of the colors and directions associated with their individual altars. These sticks were usually less than an inch in diameter, approximately four feet high, held erect in sand filled coffee canisters. In addition to the spirit-robes, prayer-ties were always displayed around them forming a rectangle with the shaman in the center of their altars. Eagle feathers and other sacred implements were displayed on dirt collected from a mole mound creating a raised surface nearby. The color and number of ties were as usual per the request of each shaman's spiritual helpers. Black Elk usually tied one hundred and fifty red ties along with a specific smaller quantity on a different string requiring specific help for himself or the patient. Red Buffalo was usually required by his spirit helpers to tie 405 prayer-ties, rotating each of the colors until all were tied on a single string. Also other colored strings of prayer ties were added if necessary. The sacred songs were selected by each shaman as their spirit helpers requested for a specific result. These were different than those sung at a yuwipi. Sixteen songs were usually sung. That amount could vary. These songs were always accompanied by at least one drum, and sometimes several. A singer or several singers would assist the shaman in this manner. As usual, when no singers were available they were sung by the wichasa wakan himself. A Chanunpa was shared by all the participants after each ceremony was completed. The "sacred mystery powers" were set in motion if all factors were in harmony.

"The thunder beings live in the West. When they come with help for someone you will often see little lightnings flying around. Spirit gave me a stone for that. The spirits say the power of Grandfather and Grandmother is a lightning," Black Elk stated to me after one of our teaching sessions related to this matter. He reminded me often about the importance of being very specific with the requests that I made of the powers. He cited an instance when a shaman had not been specific back on his reservation. Apparently the shaman had completed a ceremony to ask for more water from the skies for the crops during an extended drought. What came was hail in the form of baseballs. Cars were damaged all over the reservation as well as crops. "Grandson, this is very serious business we are involved with. Be specific with each of your words in ceremony. A sacred man speaks very slowly because he knows how important each word can be. Your spiritual intent is extremely important. That is what allows the powers to help. It is an immeasurable force which you will understand after your own path takes shape. Be patient. It takes many years to fully understand these ways."

CHAPTER 17
MEDICINE STONE

As the days, weeks, months, and years rolled by me, I let go of my preconceived notions regarding what was possible and what was not. I experienced aspects of the "Sacred Way" that most people would simply not believe. These made my walk in the mainstream world somewhat precarious. Somehow that became a special piece to the teaching that Black Elk and Red Buffalo had offered me. I was travelling on new ground walking in both worlds with balance after several years of being a Chanunpa-carrier. I was a full time Dad and husband as well as a full time sacred man.

This document is designed to be a record of this unusual teaching and practices. Perhaps some young shaman or physicist will find it useful. The story of how I received my first "medicine stone" may get their attention. There have been other stones that have come to my altar in this manner in ceremony witnessed by other participants.

As the Supervising Park Ranger of a major lake near San Diego I lived with my family in a house overlooking the water at the entrance to the camping facility that I managed. I had set up a small tipi in our back yard for my boys to play in. It also could be utilized for my private Chanunpa sessions at my home.

The universe seemed to shift for me in those moments. I was facing East. It was late afternoon. The sun was already dropping in the sky to the West towards the vast Pacific Ocean. Though the entire event lasted only seconds, my own spirit helpers did not allow me to miss what occurred. I felt as though I was in some sort of slow motion aspect of this "Sacred Way". After putting away my Chanunpa after a prayer and meditation session, directly in front of me a stone hovered in mid-air at my eye level, perhaps two feet away. It hung there several seconds so I could not miss its appearance. It then dropped to the ground at my feet where I was sitting. My initial thought was that somehow someone had thrown a stone my direction. As I pondered the moment further I realized no one could have produced the unusual hovering of that stone and then its dropping ever so gently where I sat. Still I looked around and found no one there.

When I overcame my astonishment I picked up the stone. It seemed warm to the touch. I found it had a triangular shape projecting itself from another slightly larger triangular body that fit perfectly in the palm of my hand. Some might have imagined it to be some exotic mineral or some fantastic color. It is neither of those. It is a simple deep shade of gray and feels heavy for its size. Grandfather Black Elk had spoken to me about stones that could fly as part of my training. "Takuskanskan is the mysterious power that makes things move in our universe. It can cause a stone to fly Grandson." Though I had not expressed any doubts about this to him, I wondered how such an event could take place. I couldn't wait to tell him about the incident. I shared the information with no other being, not even my wife. As serendipity would have it he was scheduled to stay over with us a few weeks later.

I went over each second of the event with him as it had transpired. A stone had appeared before me out of thin air, as he had said was possible. He and Red Buffalo had claimed that it was common knowledge among the veteran shamans that stones had the ability to "move about". Mine had appeared before me out of the ethers and dropped to the ground. I was so excited I had the stone in my hands and showed it to him immediately. It was not an illusion. I was holding it up for him to see and I saw the twinkle in his eyes after I finished my story. It felt as though I had passed another test in my spiritual training. "It has come to help you with this spiritual work," he stated with a somber look. I was disappointed that was all he had to say. After several minutes of silence he added, "You must honor this stone by wrapping it in eagle down feathers. You should store it within a special pouch or wrap it in an animal hide. That stone-person will someday reveal to you why it has come." Perhaps in the future physicists will understand the science behind *takuskanskan*. For now it remains a part of the Great Mystery.

I preserved the stone in the manner Grandfather suggested and held onto it for many years. I utilized it in my own ceremonies when that stone-person advised. Many seasons passed with its use in this manner. Recently that stone-person advised me in a special ceremony for help and health for my youngest Grandson, that it was to be given to him to help him become strong and healthy after his extremely premature birth. He was born one pound two ounces. After a lengthy stay at our University of Washington hospital he is doing well. The stone-person stayed with him at the hospital until he and it were able to come home.

There were many moments when we thought we were going to lose him. During one of these events I was asked to do a Chanunpa ceremony for him during which another ally asked me to find a feather they had left for him on the beach that sits beneath my house. They explained during that time I was to bring that feather to his hospital room to help his under-developed lungs continue to function. He is a remarkable young boy.

CHAPTER 18
INITIATION

Under the heat of the Egyptian winter sun Cairo's bustling marketplace was overflowing with activity. Bargain shoppers and locals seeking their daily nourishment brushed shoulders with Grandfather Black Elk and I as we moved through the sea of humanity surrounding us. Food vendors grilled meats with delicious smelling aromas. Freshly skinned animals were being offered for sale while hanging from storefronts. The heavy scent of brewed coffee beans vented from the coffeehouses. We rested at one and ordered a couple of shots of caffeine laced espresso that made our thick campfire brews seem week by comparison. Smoke from hookah pipes drifted above tents in the narrow winding alleyways around us. Many people were enjoying an after meal tobacco break. I chuckled at myself as I remembered learning how to smoke. The streets and narrow passageways snaked around mosques and other sandstone buildings. Cairo was a blending of the ancient and the modern. The area we were in had served as a stopover for caravans passing through on the Silk Road. Sales-people haggled in caftans, business suits, blue jeans, and t-shirts. Egyptian music spilled out of the cafes. Grandfather told me he was looking for a special drum that his spirit helpers had advised him to purchase. He mentioned perhaps a goat skin stretched over a pot. Techno-music served as a backdrop to the ancient scene before us. Vendors sold leather goods, silver and copper wares, jewelry, rugs, modern clothing, and colorful textiles from the African continent. As I looked in each direction I saw old, young, black, white, Arab, Asian, Middle-Eastern, and Western people, including a robust Native American with a grin on his face.

I was excited and oddly nervous about what Grandfather Black Elk told me would take place inside the Great Pyramid. I had experienced many extraordinary moments over my years of doing ceremony with him in different environments. My own spirit helpers advised me to prepare for something special.

He had been invited to give a lecture to an Earth Conference of people from around the world that would take place on the grounds of the Great Pyramids in Giza, Egypt. The facilitator of the event had made the proper arrangements with the government so as to allow different groups to utilize the interior of that sacred space with no tourist interruptions during several half-day meditations.

During one of Grandfather Black Elk's stays with us at my lake assignment, he asked me if I might be interested in going to help him in Egypt with the drumming and sacred singing. "It will be an opportunity for you to experience Egypt and do ceremony in one of the most sacred temples in the world. There will be many types of healers there and many who care about the Earth Mother with the same compassion we have." I told him I had always been especially curious about the Great Pyramids and their builders. "The Egyptians did purification ceremonies not in stone-people-lodges like us, but in stone buildings that can still be found outside those pyramids," he added. "I am looking forward to seeing what those are like."

I flew from San Diego to meet Grandfather Black Elk in New York and we proceeded to Paris, France for a brief layover, and then on to Cairo, Egypt. He had been more talkative than usual and chatted about many subjects while we were in the air. He reminded me he was a scout in Egypt in WWII, and had spent time in the deserts outside the area of the Great Pyramids with a small group of men who had parachuted in to scout out enemy movements.

"The stone-people that I carry in this leather pouch on my belt are the same 'stone-people' I carried in the war. On several occasions these stones saved my life and others with their communication to me that enemy soldiers were approaching. My men and I survived because of these stones. We made it through some very dangerous experiences," he reminisced. The pouch of stones that he spoke about had always intrigued me.

I told him I had been doing a bit of research prior to our travel and that the three Great Pyramids had been estimated to be built with approximately fifteen million tons of stone. "That is a lot of rocks, Grandfather," I said as we burst into laughter together. They had been conventionally attributed to pharaohs Khufu, Khafre, and Menkaure. "Nothing about them appears accidental, their original heights, their angles of slope, the measurements of their perimeters, even their pattern on the earth all contain special meaning in relationship of distance and size to the moon and other heavenly bodies. The Great Pyramid was originally about four hundred and eighty feet high. It is now reduced to around four hundred and fifty feet high."

"Grandson, I remember seeing them only from the outside during the war."

I went on while looking at some notes I had made, "The Great Pyramid's four sides each measure about seven hundred and fifty-five feet in length at their bases. The second tallest pyramid was slightly lower at around four hundred and seventy feet high with its base a little over seven hundred feet. The third tallest pyramid stands around two hundred and fifteen feet tall with a base of a little over three hundred and fifty feet. When they were built the largest two were completely covered in limestone and no doubt were spectacular in the Egyptian sunshine. Only a few sections still remain," I explained. "Striation marks alongside the sphinx and pyramids have caused scientists to date them back at least as far as the last great flood of 10,500 years ago. Local historians have resisted this new data."

"More astounding than the mass and size of these structures is the incredible precision in which they are built. In the early 70's under the guidance of Japanese technicians a very small pyramid was attempted. It was to be built to emulate the way the pyramids had been constructed. However, no machine from our technological era could move anything that massive. Nothing could cut it and put it into place like a pyramid. Their attempt had created something pathetic in comparison." Grandfather felt right at home in the smoke filled cabin during our lengthy flight. However, my lungs began to suffer not being conditioned to that kind of air quality.

Upon our arrival in Egypt we secured a taxi and checked into our hotel room located within walking distance of the Giza necropolis. It had served as a palace long ago and many of its ornate furnishings were still intact. We shared the room there to minimize our costs for our journey.

Special groupings of large tents set up outside the pyramids were in place for the conference. Those colorful temporary structures handled hundreds of people easily and had done so historically in that desert when needed.

In the few days before our anticipated ceremony, we enjoyed exploring the surrounding area. At the museum in Cairo we were particularly impressed by the features of Isis depicted most often as a winged being. She appeared angel-like. We viewed many winged beings throughout the enormity of their collection of antiquities and

Grandfather seemed particularly intrigued by them. Perhaps he knew some things he had not divulged to me about our futures.

During our exploring of the countryside we viewed life along the Nile that is still very dependent on its flooding cycles for farming. Donkeys attached to carts filled with people are still driven on their busy roads as automobiles squeeze past processions of many groups of families walking to the marketplace.

The Sphinx was covered with scaffolding to help preserve parts that were deteriorating. I found it very powerful even with the maintenance going on. I marveled at the majesty of that part lion, part human virgin and wondered why it had been constructed and by whom.

One evening we continued our search for Grandfather's Egyptian drum. We finally were forced to give up after our taxi came to rest with all doors scraping the stone structures along the winding narrow alleyway we had taken. The driver had to back out scraping each side of his vehicle or we would still be there hopelessly stuck not able to open any doors. We detoured to another area where he purchased some ancient scents at the perfume shops that his spirit helpers advised could be used in his work.

Because of Grandfathers status we were honored guests at several receptions during our stay. At these we were served many local delicacies and I never knew exactly what we were eating because of the language barrier. It all tasted quite spicy and scented the air with flavors unknown to me. Eventually lentil soup became my main staple as I tried to impose a moderate fast prior to my entry into the Great Pyramid.

One of our favorite activities while waiting for our ceremony was riding camels in the desert. Lawrence of Arabia would have been proud. It amazed me how perfectly suited the camels were to that harsh environment. Though you lurch with each camel step they are quite fast traveling over sand when they want to be. On our short rides away from civilization I found it very easy to believe all the stories about people getting lost out in that wilderness. While exploring each of the smaller pyramids we found the inner rectangular space of the second largest pyramid to be the most interesting. We completed about an hour meditation inside that space.

Finally it was our time to enter the Great Pyramid we had come for. I carried Grandfather's drum and my Chanunpa and he transported his "medicine suitcase" filled with all his ceremonial implements. We had been cautioned by Egyptian authorities that absolutely no fire was permitted inside. "Having no fire inside will not be a problem, Grandson. There is something else that my spirit helpers have shared with me that I want you to know. This sacred architecture causes a special awareness utilized by others like us throughout its history. It has been used for sacred ceremony by many shamans down through the ages. That includes the man the Christians called Jesus." He laughed and grinned from ear to ear drawing further attention to his remark knowing the background I had been raised in.

" I have heard the effects within this structure have to do with where the chambers are located within the sacred geometry of the pyramid itself," I added. "Many experiments have been done within pyramid shapes. Dull razor blades turn sharp after a short period of time within. Cut flowers stay fresh long after the same flowers stored outside a pyramid have withered."

He nodded and added, "Pyramid means 'fire in the middle' and the light that each of us is made of is rearranged inside this sacred architecture. It makes sense that a shaman would have a special affinity for these fiery shapes."

The Great Pyramid is an elaborate arrangement of passageways and galleries sloping at twenty-six degree angles ascending and descending to the inner chambers. There are three primary chambers that we had access to.

We explored the subterranean chamber first. After gaining access to the descending corridor we climbed up to an iron grille that blocks off the true entrance located in the monument's North face. The entrance we entered through was broken into years ago and is called Mamoun's hole. With our backs bent we hunched over and continued down into the bedrock of the Giza plateau along a 350 foot corridor at that same uncomfortable 26 degree angle. When you are there you do not realize you are about 600 feet below the pyramids lofty summit. This space seemed horribly contaminated with tourist energies, and the smell of urine was quite prevalent.

As we moved gradually up towards the King's Chamber I realized my legs felt like rubber and I was concerned about Grandfather. It was a rigorous climb especially with all of our sacred implements. At times the stairs turned to stone inclines with wooden slats to keep us from sliding backwards. The sour smells disappeared as we ascended.

On our stone path to the King's Chamber the ceiling was so low we both had to crouch and drag along our ceremonial implements in a modified duck waddle. Some places were a little over three feet by three feet by my visual estimation. These were barely passable for large human beings.

Connecting this passageway to the Kings Chamber is the grand gallery a corbel vaulted hall over 150 feet in length and seven feet in width. Its height is almost 30 feet and this space was a relief to enter prior to our entrance into the flat roofed Kings Chamber itself. A few low wattage bulbs installed in modern times revealed the inner stones massive qualities and textures. Upon entering we discovered a red granite room rectangular in shape.

It measures approximately 34 feet in length by 17 feet in width and a little less than 20 feet to the ceiling, and is all stone. It is located about 150 feet above the outside base of the structure.

A stone sepulchre sat at one end of the space just long enough for a man to lie in. Its top piece apparently disappeared years ago. Its whereabouts are unknown. After we tested the inside of this stone rectangle Black Elk felt it had been utilized in some ancient form of vision-quest. "Some Lakota family's still utilized vision quest pits not much larger than that," he reminded me.

I could feel the energy shift as each member of our group went into their meditative silence. Grandfather Black Elk and I laid our Chanunpas out in the very center of that space. A drizzle of sweat ran down my brow as I took out what we would need for our time there. I suppressed a cough as I contemplated the lack of oxygen within the stone walls.

Ancient Egyptians attributed their civilization to the gods who came in what they called "the first time", Zep Tepi. A sense of mystery of the sublime filled me while preparing for our ceremony. Could those ancient master builders have found a way to initiate those of us to come thousands of years later by making use of the stars in alignment with this space? Was it true that the air ducts line up to the stars in the constellation of Orion where the builders came from originally? These were questions I pondered as I sat next to a standing Black Elk in that great stone chamber. He was taking the scene in for what seemed to be a very acute altered awareness. There must have been approximately 20 others from the Earth Conference who had asked to be part of our group inside the pyramid.

Everyone settled into as comfortable a position as they could against the stone walls that surrounded us in each direction. Grandfather Black

Elk and I were in the center of the floor of that King's Chamber, within that rectangle of people. The crystal healer had already arranged the area in front of her with her crystals. The Egyptian tarot specialist volunteered to be in charge of going down the passageway to turn off all of the primitive electric lights. Another Chanunpa-carrier was going to help with the drumming and singing once we began. We were in complete darkness. It reminded me of the black light within a stone-people-lodge. It was so black I could not see my hand in front of my body.

Black Elk asked me to utilize his eagle fan to cleanse all of the participants in our circle. He emphasized I needed to vigorously fan away any negative energies left inside our makeshift circle as we would not be using our sage or sweet grass within the chamber. Each person acknowledged the fanning as a special blessing as I moved around the enclosure. Grandfather said a prayer and we began to drum and sing several sacred songs. After a pause and more songs, the floor seemed to be moving underneath me. It was vibrating as if we were in an earthquake.

Next I heard Black Elk saying something I could not make out in Lakota, after which he handed me his pouch of stones. They were beating like two hearts. I was not hallucinating. The stones he handed me had heart beats. It was the first time I had been allowed to handle the stones in the leather pouch he most often wore attached to his belt. I wondered if they would help us in that sacred chamber when I laid them by our Chanunpas in the very center of that room. Our drum beat and singing sounded exceptional within the confines of that natural sound chamber. Oddly enough my mind shifted to a conversation I had with Red Buffalo after we first met about tipis and pyramids being part of a sacred geometry.

After our last song a silence set in and then I could hear the beat of wings flapping way off in the distance. I could make out spirit eagles and hawks high above us inside the darkness. I could see their ethereal red and blue forms. I remember seeing the shape of a spirit buffalo. Its large form passed in front of me. The next thing I remember I saw were shapes of spirit dolphins. They came, swimming through the air, beginning at the stone ceiling. They were light blue ethereal dolphins swimming in the air. A wolf shape moved through the wall to my right side. Globes of white light about the size of basketballs floated for a time near the ceiling and then they became separated like confetti floating down to the stone floor.

I had lost track of normal time. Had I been transported into another realm? It seemed as if one moment I was totally immersed in the singing we had performed inside the Kings Chamber of the Great Pyramid, and the next instant she had appeared before me. I immediately became aware of the serene energy her feminine shape projected. A gentle calm filled me. I sat up in anticipation on the stone floor. She was beautiful. Her hair was a golden yellow. It had reminded me of those haystacks in the summer fields in the valley town of my birth. It hung gracefully over her shoulders where her wings moved ever so slowly like a butterfly leaving the safety of its cocoon for the very first time. They were motionless for a few seconds as she pointed them above me towards what would have been the sky. Instead I was reminded of the stone ceiling above where I was sitting. Could this really be an angel in front of me?

I could only slightly make out the shape of her eyes, nose, and chin, when she first appeared. She radiated an ethereal blue light like the space inside a movie theatre when total darkness is interrupted with reflected light off the big screen. She towered above me as I sat in awe. I estimated her height at about ten feet. White layered robes flowed from her shoulders to the floor of the pyramids. They touched my moccasins in real space.

I stared into her eyes and she looked down at mine and she began to communicate to me. "Greetings to you, son of Imhotep." As she stood before me I bowed my head and she blessed me with her feathers. She lightly brushed my head, my face, and my shoulders, down to my heart with her wing tips. "I am honored to meet you." I whispered. I could feel those feathers in real time. This was not a dream.

"Many truths will be sought and found by human beings as you near the end of this fourth Great Age of Mankind. Human beings will soon have an opportunity to move forward from one level of consciousness to another in a higher octave. War, strife, and discord are but outer manifestations of a civilization whose delusions are nearing their end. Listen to your heart for the voice of truth and hope. Each being carries a drop of divine intelligence, you are each a part of the undying flame. Remain in service to all beings on life's circle and peace and harmony will come."

There was a long pause and then she stated this: "Mankind has created many sorrows. Try not to be discouraged. Look within and always be reminded of who you are. It is there the radiance of Great Spirit shines through to all that you meet."

She then spoke to me about my family... my job...where I lived...and then she added this about my future, "Possible perils await you on your home-front. Consider raising your family where you will find the sacred peace while living under the tall trees, in the clean air, and by the flowing waters of a northern ground." After another lengthy silence, she sang me a song. When it was over she explained I would remember the song to help me remember her words. She said I could use it in my own ceremonies to ask for help when I needed it. The next thing I remember is that she no longer occupied that space with me.

Questions swam through my mind like a pod of orca whales surfacing above reality only to splash again into three-dimensional waters. What had the others experienced during my encounter with the angel? Why was I feeling totally debilitated? It took all of the energy I could muster just to move a very few steps. As I paused to gain my composure I realized most of the others in our group had left. Sun Bear, another native elder who I had admired greatly before our journey, said congratulations to me and left for his hotel. I was able to focus again on the interior space. He seemed to know I had been through something major. Was this part of an initiation of some sort?

I found Grandfather still in an altered state of consciousness a few paces away. He was also moving very slowly. Several people were around him talking. I wandered slowly to the Queen's Chamber to meditate on what had just occurred. Spirit seemed to be directing me there for some sort of decompression activity. A healer from Canada was singing a beautiful song in that chamber. I wept.

I then glimpsed Grandfather Black Elk in the passageway coming for me. It was time to depart. We were each trying to cope with what we had just experienced. I did not know then that he had seen and talked to his own angel. We barely made it back to our sleeping quarters before total exhaustion leveled me. I felt like I was about to pass out prior to my head hitting my pillow. I did not stir at all until 12 hours had passed by. Grandfather was still asleep in his bed when I arose.

Societies and civilizations around the globe have recorded stories about angel encounters. I had never given any thought to actually seeing one let alone having this kind of communication between us.

The song she left me with is very dear to my heart. I have utilized that song when I need her help in my own ceremonies.

*Please note that my angel also brings up the next Great Age of Mankind. Many indigenous societies believe we are in that process currently as signaled by events over the last several years.

CHAPTER 19
ANCIENT MYSTERY

The following day I awoke to a feeling of overwhelming joy. I experienced the awareness that I had been initiated into the great mystery of a Sacred Way. The scene had been facilitated by a sacred man and overseen by my angel. I pondered what she had said about moving my family North by the big trees, clean air, and flowing water as I lay in my bed trying to gather my energy.

And how would I find this place? What perils existed at our home? I contemplated why had she called me son of Imhotep? Grandfathers advice to me about not always asking why, now made me laugh out loud. We eventually revealed to each other that we had each seen and talked with what we both described as angels. We then took turns describing portions of what we experienced. Laughter then filled the air once again. Grandfather had that twinkle in his eyes. He admitted he was still dazzled by his encounter with a beautiful brown skinned being with long black hair. He estimated his angel was approximately 10 feet tall, with a wing span that stretched another 6 to 8 feet above her. I described my angel to him and we compared the similarities and differences. He was quite intrigued that my angel had given me a song to help me remember her words and realize it was not a dream. I sang it for him then and blinked a lot to try to hold back my tears. I could see he was moved by the song and also too choked up to speak. I could also see how exhausted he still was. I excused myself for the day to find some quiet time and let him nap. We met up that night over a quiet dinner. The effects of that space had not worn off. I wonder if they ever will?

I arranged our plans for the following day. The place we would explore next was Saqqara. "The famous 'pyramid texts' are carved on the walls there," I reminded him at our breakfast. We had regained some of our energy. "Saqqara is about ten miles to the south of us here at Giza so it won't take us long to get there. I will grab a cab for us after we are finished here."

It had apparently been a major surprise for people to discover that the ancient inscriptions, thought originally to have been done by farmers of the fifth and sixth dynasty, had spoken often about iron. They describe an ancient star gate leading to the celestial belt of Orion. I thought about that iron star gate throughout my day. The claim sounded right out of a science fiction movie.

During our drive to the Step Pyramid of Zoser, Grandfather was silent. At first glance I remember thinking it appeared to be quite rudimentary in all aspects of its design in comparison to the Great Pyramid. Rather than a smooth surface running from an apex to the four sides of a base, the step pyramid had different ascending levels leading to a flat surface at its peak. Though we never stepped a foot inside this structure we explored its exterior ruins and found them to be quite fascinating. The rainbow colored hieroglyphs on the walls of the adjoining structures were beautiful and contained more impressive colors than I thought would remain after who knew how many years.

We wandered throughout the outer structures and columns that were adjacent to the Step Pyramid of Zoser that afternoon. Black Elk and I sang several sacred songs in the main courtyard. I became overwhelmed with the emotions of the day before. My eyes glistened after we sang the sacred song he had been teaching me in the months before our trip. His eyes were moist as well. A Grandfather and his Grandson were overcome with the power of it all.

Something momentous had occurred again on this miraculous Sacred Way I was now merged with.

Grandfather requested I invite any of those from our group that we had seen on the grounds that day, who wished to participate in a Chanunpa ceremony, to join us in the desert outside of the pyramid complex. After wandering around on foot in the open desert, he chose a section of sand about one hundred yards from the Pyramid. He asked me to smudge that area with sage and sweet grass, including those people who had joined us.

He and I filled our Chanunpas and offered them to Great Spirit and the six directions. We sang several sacred songs. He next made an unusual request of me. He asked for me to dig several inches under the sand where we sat. He explained to me that I would find tiny stones buried at about eight to twelve inches underneath that sandy soil. Beneath those stones I would find burnt wheat. Grandfather's spirit helpers were again correct. Those stones were about the size of the heads of a typical eight penny nail. They were scattered evenly throughout the areas I dug in. He asked me to retrieve several of these for our medicine bags. They were round, off white in color, with an unusual agate look to them. "The Spirits call this place Imhotep's launching ground", he said in an unusual tone. I was stunned to hear him bring up the same name my angel had used. I paused for a few moments to catch my breath. I had not mentioned that name relating to my angel encounter to him. "They say this man led many people to a new home from here." I wondered what it could all mean.

We sang several more songs and smoked our Chanunpas with the entire circle of new friends.

I had filled my Chanunpa with prayers of thanks. We completed our ceremony with a group hug. Then what happened seemed a perfect ending to our time in Egypt. It began to rain. It rained only about fifty yards in every direction right over our heads. I had seen it rain after certain rituals we had accomplished together, and knew this was one of the skills Grandfather possessed regarding the natural world and this Sacred Way. After sprinkling on us for several minutes our baptism seemed complete. There had not been a sign of rain our entire stay. No one else got rain that day as far as I know. We adjourned back to our hotel via taxi in silence.

I looked forward to my return to my family. I had no idea how I would share my unusual news.

CHAPTER 20
RED HAWK

I've admired them for many years. Sometimes they are perched at the tops of bare trees. Sometimes they are hunched on fence posts after a soaking rain. Other times I see them soaring against the sun and a clear cerulean blue sky. At times they are like missiles shooting down through space to acquire their next meal. While deep in forests I have seen them darting between branches with great speed and dexterity. They glide slowly over my head. It seems like they are wherever I am. It is an unusual part of this Sacred Way. When I think of a friend many times I hear that friend has just seen a Red Hawk.

I see them in dream-time . When I am there I can hear their piercing cries. I sometimes feel for a few heartbeats that I am soaring with them. I can literally feel the tug of a rising thermal and glimpse the earth from afar. My head feels light. I am confident and coordinated in my new movements through space. My eyes grow huge and become fixed to each side of my head so I can see all around me quite easily. My body feels the muscles and organs located near my center. I am healthy and compact. My wings unfurl and my legs are tucked close to my body. My blood pressure is high and pumping energy throughout my new shape. I feel my lungs fill deeply with air. I am explosive and powerful. When I open my wings I can literally hop into the wind. I am hovering in my extra light body. I can sense the hollow aspects of my bones and feathers. I digest and excrete my food as I have no bladder. I feel perfectly light and effortless. As I ride a burst of wind I can feel the air stream over my extended wings. My smaller feathers buffer any turbulence. I can feel the lifting force pull me up from above. I can sense the rigidity of my spine to center my sturdy aircraft. I am able to pump my wings to increase my speed. Oxygen soaks into my body as I steer with my tail and wing feathers. Soaring…soaring…soaring….I love to soar. I make a wide sweep to my left. Then I slowly make a wide sweep to my right. As I begin to descend I recall my human shape… I can feel again the weight of my arms and legs and torso. I have become a humble man again. I love that too.

Wallace Black Elk said these words to me on the day of my naming ceremony, "Grandson, you have a new name, you are 'Red Hawk', *Che-tan Lu-ta*." That was all he said, but he was smiling broadly. I think he liked it. Much later, when I asked my spirit helpers in an inipi ceremony what my new name meant, they stated, "A Red Hawk is capable of flying high with the eagles to see great distances. It can even see into the future. A Red Hawk is also capable of maneuvering with quick turns in tight quarters and is very capable of making good decisions in the moment. The red symbolizes fire which represents the living spirit of the people. This fire resides within you."

I remember fondly all the raptors I was able to rehabilitate and then release into the wild while still a ranger. The two red hawks that I handled most because of their large populations in that area were red-tailed hawks and red-shouldered hawks.

Red-tailed hawks are one of the largest members of the genus buteo. They roughly weigh one to four pounds and measure eighteen to twenty-six inches in length with a wingspan of between forty-three and fifty-seven inches. There plumage is variable based on their subspecies of dark, light, and rufus. Their basic appearance includes a lighter underbelly than their backs with a dark band across their bellies forming horizontal streaks in feather patterning. Their red tails are uniformly brick red above with pink below. Their bills are short and dark with a hooked shape. Their legs and feet are yellow and their eyes range from yellow in the immature birds to reddish brown in the adults.

Red-shouldered hawks are a medium sized member of the genus buteo. They roughly weigh one to two pounds and measure eighteen to twenty-four inches in length with a wing span of thirty-eight to forty-one inches. Their basic appearance includes brownish toned heads, reddish chests, and pale bellies with reddish bars. Their tails are longer than red-tailed hawks marked with narrow white bars. Their upper parts are dark with pale spots. They also have yellow legs and the same eye hues.

On one occasion, as I went to free a red-shouldered hawk by tossing it into the air after a successful rehabilitation, the magnificent bird dug both talons into my forearms. With blood streaming down both arms like a pierced Sun Dancer, I managed to pry him loose and got him air born. My naming ceremony brought that creature clearly into focus. This Sacred Way is a great mystery.

Typically a naming ceremony happens during the daylight, not at the usual hours of dusk, as in most stone-people-lodge ceremonies. Twenty friends and family were in attendance that day. Grandfather explained that the Spirits would know me as Red Hawk from that point forward.

CHAPTER 21
BLACK ELK TEACHINGS: VIEJAS RESERVATION

The Viejas Band of Kumeyaay Native Americans, one of the remaining twelve bands of that nation, reside on a 1,600 acre area in the Viejas Valley about thirty minutes drive from my last park assignment at Lake Jennings. The Kumeyaay were the original inhabitants of San Diego County, California. They believe they have inhabited that region for over 10,000 years. Their lands once extended from the Pacific Ocean South to Mexico, East to the sand dunes of Colorado, and North to the territory of the Warner Springs Valley in the vicinity of my previous park assignment at Wilderness Gardens.

They hunted game ranging from rabbit and quail, to antelope and deer. They fished their inland rivers and the sea. They made fine woven baskets, pottery, clothing, and shelters that varied based on the seasons. When the Spanish first saw the meadows of the Kumeyaay they assumed they were natural, when in fact they were viewing grain fields that had been planted and irrigated. They were considered some of the best environmental managers of North America. Beginning with the Spanish invasion in 1709 their lands were reduced over many years. Because of Grandfather's reputation we were allowed access to an area not far from where Viejas Casino was built several years later after our stone-people-lodge was dismantled after my move out of that area.

After our Great Pyramid experience, each stone-people-lodge ceremony we accomplished together, offered another piece to the knowledge puzzle he and Red Buffalo had solved for me. He explained to me that in the Lakota wichasa wakan tradition, I would notice levels of power in four year segments, or four times four-season segments, followed by a leap to a new octave regarding the "sacred mystery powers" acquired, followed by another, and another. The first four years seemed to be so jammed with knowledge acquisition that I felt I had completed some sort of expedited training regimen.

In his next level of teaching with me, Grandfather seemed extremely careful. I believe he attempted to make sure I had grasped a concept before moving on in his hope of directing me out of harm's way. I felt as though I needed to be even more aware in the realms I travelled because something ominous out there was more aware of my presence.

"The Lakota often choose their words carefully because we know how powerful words can become. In the beginning was the black light, living darkness, the ancient Grandmother. Out of this Tunkashila brought fire. Fire is the essence of spirit and life at the heart of everything. It is awesome power. Fire is also represented by the sun. The sun is the source of life. Next Tunkashila created rock. Rocks are the body of Grandmother Earth. The stone nations are the oldest beings on this planet. Grandson, you now have an awareness of how powerful stones can be. When they come into our stone-people-lodge ceremonies they function as messengers from Great Spirit." Grandfather's mental thunder echoed in the air. "Then Tunkashila created water and covered the earth with it. Water is the sacred substance that supports all life. Finally Tunkashila created the green which includes as a general category both the plant and animal kingdoms. I am reminding you of our creation story because when we put our Chanunpas together in our ceremonies, the stone bowls and the wood stems of our Chanunpas, and we fill them with green, our chashasha mixture of herbs and tobacco, we create the smoke that connects us to the spiritual realm. We have added fire to our prayers. We have added our breath to those prayers. We have offered Tunkashila well-chosen and precise words. We bring those powers of creation forward with our good intentions and with the help of our spiritual helpers. What we have created is a sacred alchemy." An aura of power pervaded the camp fire as He and I sat and listened to the crackle and pop of the sap filled wood in silence into the wee hours of that night.

On another occasion while preparing for a group of Native Americans from that reservation he had this to say to me. "It makes me happy to hear you sing our ceremonial songs. You have come far in a short time." As he paused my thoughts drifted to our final ceremony at the Great Pyramid. The entire conference formed a procession to walk in single file around the ancient structure. We each lit a candle at each of the cardinal points of the four corners of the pyramid and said a prayer for humankind's relationship to the Earth Mother. Where we had begun our walk, the procession formed a serpentine body of over a hundred people around Grandfather and I singing and praying at his drum. It was an exquisite scene with many people from all corners of the earth sharing the Lakota honoring song he had taught me in the months prior to our going there. "I see that you have utilized the words from the songs that you now know to help you understand more and more of my language. The Lakota language has at its roots a universal language. That language recognizes and respects the communication of all beings, human and non-human alike. In our language everything is scientific, logical, fluent, and integrated. There is no profanity because we know that all things are sacred. My teachers taught me, as I have taught you, that the Earth People, not just the Lakota, all of the people of our planet, were given one drop of knowledge from the Earth Mother and one drop of wisdom from Creator, Great Spirit. These two merge into one force to produce the power a sacred man uses to help others. You have become very aware of the power that we walk with. You now understand the transformational ability of fire. The result for a wichasa wakan regarding this alchemical process is the talent to accomplish many expressions of this Sacred Way. Always remember that that power is a gift from Great Spirit. It is not ours. To utilize this gift a person should come to you with a tobacco offering or some part of the plant nation to ask for your help. They must ask in this manner for you to know they are sincere in their need."

"Nineteen generations ago there was a great meeting of the people of Turtle Island. At that time everyone spoke the same language. It was a form of the universal language I mentioned earlier. The purpose of that gathering was to assure that everyone unanimously understood the same sacred ceremonies that I have taught you. Those ceremonies through which men and women could communicate in a sacred manner with each other and all the other animal, vegetable, and mineral nations. At that time Tunkashila had instructed the people to come together every seven generations to reaffirm their unity and understanding of these ways."

"It was agreed that there must be a thorough examination of any doubts or shadows in people's minds. The gathering was supposed to continue until there was unanimous understanding again. Prophecies received at that time foretold of a time in the future when tremendous dissonance would prevail upon the Earth Mother and then the people would come forth once again to share these sacred ways to help prevent a planet wide disaster. Many Earth People have lost their way. Many other peoples on the earth have lost their way. As the world teeters on an apocalyptic ending I am still hopeful that many others will awaken to a more conscious sense of responsibility. We are spirit moving through these human forms. People need to once again demonstrate in the way they live what it is like to be alive and well in spirit."

"Grandson, when we were in Egypt together you saw that one of the families that had cared for the Great Pyramid's grounds gifted me an Egyptian Chanunpa. They told us it was very old. I want you to understand clearly that there was a time on the planet when all nations understood the power of the Sacred Pipe. Not just the red nation. All the human families utilized this sacred tool to communicate with Spirit. That Chanunpa they gifted me is based on a design from an even earlier period of time. It was made from pottery and wood. I also want you to realize how long people have been using their stone-people-lodges on this planet of ours. I am happy we got to see an Egyptian stone house there that was utilized as a purification lodge. These exist at most pyramid sites around the world."

At another teaching session he had this to say. "During our ceremony inside the Great Pyramid my spirit helpers confirmed that those structures are ancient. They are much older than the Egyptian historians let on. They are thousands of years off on the calculations for when they were built. They are even older than our present day scientists have predicted. They are remnants of another Great Age of Mankind. My Spirit helpers explained to me that a whistle-like device was utilized to cut and move the stones. It had an anti-gravity effect on those massive stone-people. They also said that a race from beyond the sun helped design and build those structures and that those star people had a great deal to do with our advancement. As

I have shared with you before, many of our sacred men and women have gone up on a hill to accomplish their hanbleychas and been contacted by the star- people. It has happened to me on more than one occasion. They explained to me that someday solar activity from the sun will likely cause a massive electrical outage on the Earth Mother. None of our electrical devices will work during this time. They did not say exactly when or how long this event would last."

CHAPTER 22
ANGEL DIALOGUE: CALIFORNIA

Red Hawk: When we had our visit in the sacred temple in Egypt you mentioned perils that I would have to face on the home front. Could you clarify what you meant?

Angel: He who enters the path of power that you now walk upon always faces danger in the early stages of this chosen life.

Red Hawk: How do I best conquer those forces?

Angel: Your soul is strong, but you will be tested. You may feel as if those forces are dissolving your former life. Do not live in the moment of these perils. Do not live in the future of these perils. Live in the eternal of who you have become. Your true self is much stronger than anything that could bring you harm. Because you are at the precipice of a new threshold your ordeal must be endured. It is the choice you have made. Seek your purity as you walk your new path. Be guided by your inner light.

Red Hawk: Can you be any more specific about me possibly moving my family to a more appropriate setting.

Angel: Nothing will disturb the sacred peace you seek. You will be responsible for that discovery. Your soul will grow even stronger there.

Red Hawk: Grandfather has encouraged me to do a vision quest at a traditional site in South Dakota to help me choose an appropriate path. Is this a beneficial course for me at this time?

Angel: The knowledge you gain about your true path on that mountain will allow you to move forward with your life with greater ease. However, your Sacred Way is not found through this activity by itself. Nor can it be found by spiritual practice by itself. Nor can it be found by this form of meditation by itself. Nor can it be found by observing your natural world by itself. Nor can it be found by simplifying your life by itself. Your entire nature must be utilized to transform yourself, in the same way a chrysalis becomes a butterfly. The pain of your beginning steps will act as a reminder of your awakened intent to serve others.

CHAPTER 23
BEAR BUTTE-HANBLEYCHA

Dusk was drawing its cloak across Bear Butte, *Mato Paha* , as I set up my hanbleycha site with a view toward the distant hills that rolled like an amber sea toward the horizon line. A light breeze caused the trees to rustle and acted as a cooling agent for all the unseen forces whispering their stories to me that evening. At Grandfather's urging I had come to fast and pray on one of the traditional vision quest sites for Lakota wichasa wakans. This lone mountain standing by itself above the plains of Southeast South Dakota rises above the prairie on the Northeast edge of the Black Hills. The mountain has religious significance for over thirty indigenous groups from Canada to North Texas. It is well known that Red Cloud, Crazy Horse, and Sitting Bull performed ceremonies there.

At the time of my visit it was classed as a state monument and managed as a park. During my walk up the switch backed trail to a rocky overlook, spirit-robes and prayer-ties hung casually from the pine trees like some form of mysterious ancient fruits. An occasional eagle feather had been left by former hanbleycha participants attached to hand-made choke cherry bark circles honoring the four directions. I had picked enough sage the day before to make a comfortable nest inside my own spirit-robes and prayer-ties positioned around me.

The beat of my drum and the ancient songs I sang immediately opened my soul to the heart of that land. I prayed and sang to the glory of the heavens above me as my eyes shifted to the stars that soon commanded my vision. My ears strained to hear any sounds that the Spirits might be sending. All was quiet except for the whisper of a few tree branches. After praying this way for hours, I huddled into my star blanket feeling the chill of the night air.

I had driven two thousand miles from San Diego to South Dakota to fast and pray for some direction regarding my future. Grandfather had been happy that I had brought him two full buffalo robes that he needed to fulfill a task he had received from his spirit helpers regarding the making of a family drum. We completed a purification lodge together outside of Denver with several of his friends from that area. Fools Crow's words came to me during that session, "See with your mind, touch with your eyes, and decide with your heart."

I now wept openly thinking of the time I was able to spend at Wounded Knee with Grandfather's relatives. While I was there I could still feel the sadness moving through that valley and those gullies from what had transpired almost a century before. Overhead the stars wheeled slowly on their course, eternal circle without end. They moved slowly across the night sky.

Moment by moment the world around me began to be more and more visible. I could see mists moving slowly in the distance. I focused on the bird nations now singing their songs to call up the sun. In the East the sky grew pale with a new days approach. I got up again and danced and sang and moved around my altar. As I did so the fiery disk of the sun lifted gradually above the horizon, and I lifted my Chanunpa to honor its new radiance. My drum beat died away again in a spiral of sound down the mountain. I knew that certain knowledge of what is to come is given to few people. I concentrated once more. Since dawn I had focused my prayers regarding the matter of where I should move my family. My angel had directed me North where the big trees grew, the waters flowed, and the air was clean. Washington State entered into my mind. Then my angel's voice came to me, "Listen with a quiet heart, with an open soul, without desire, and without judgment".

A short time later a different voice spoke to me, "A sacred man is like a magical bird that has paused in its reality to give man hope and purpose. He lives under the wing of that bird in the freedom of his life. Never let others tell you how the world really is."

As the heat of the day stretched before me Washington State thoughts filled me up. The shadows were beginning to lengthen and the afternoon was warm and silent when I became fixated on the clear cerulean blue sky. I had become an empty vessel waiting to be filled as I watched clouds moving slowly out of nowhere in that formerly clear space. As they coalesced directly in front of my gaze I was startled to see one, then two, then three, then four buffaloes, form in magnificent white and grey shapes. These were not abstract shapes. They were clearly buffalo. They had appeared during my thoughts about Washington State being the possible move. Then like a traveler who meets an old friend upon a road and pauses for a few moments of greeting before passing along-they disappeared.

As the sun began to set it was time to make my way off that sacred ground. My family became first and foremost on my mind. I pondered the thought of Washington State and knew that my vision of the four buffalo was meant for me to know that Washington State was where we belonged.

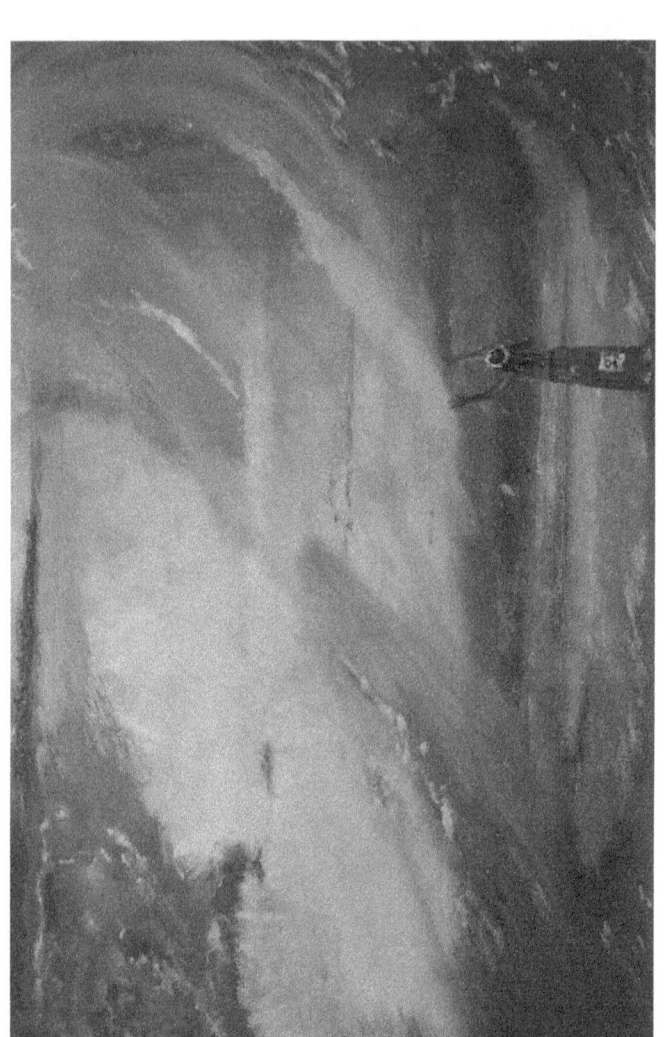

CHAPTER 24
SACRED CLOWNS-HEYOKA WICHASAS

A storm in the distance spat lightning on the far horizon over a desolate section of the Great Plains in the heartland of Turtle Island. I was traveling with another of Grandfather Black Elk's nephews Gerald to a purification lodge that we hoped we would find interesting. He announced that we had less than an hour before we needed to look for our turn off onto a dirt road in the middle of a lonely stretch of sage scrub country. Short flashes illuminated the tops of distant hills miles away. After the appropriate pause a low rumble of thunder seemed to roll through our environment in muffled rustling. Gerald and I had become *kolas*, back in San Diego where we both lived. He had come to where my family and I lived to go back to school to get his college degree. I had helped him make the necessary connections to student aid and medical coverage through local native grants. He too was receiving an education from his Uncle Wallace in the ways of the wichasa wakan. Grandfather had spent a good deal of time in our part of the country teaching and doing ceremony with us. He eventually married Gerald to a friend of ours in a traditional blanket ceremony on the Viejas Reservation near our stone-people-lodge.

Gerald's broad shoulders now slumped a bit from fatigue. His black hair hung modestly to his collar framing his round coffee toned features. He now smiled at me, revealing a strong Lakota countenance as well as the chipped teeth broken in a long forgotten fight to survive as a youth. His once broken nose added another story to his interesting history. The Spirits had named him after one of the most renowned warrior leaders in their history. He received his name Crazy Horse, *Tashunka Witko,* in a naming ceremony he had completed with his Uncle Wallace similar to my own. He had received that name after coming back from the war in Viet Nam. It was a topic he never wanted to talk about except for the fact that Black Elk had completed a special ceremony for him before he left. It included leaving his Chanunpa on a hill until Gerald got back safely. That in itself was a remarkable feat for all who participated in the combat over there. Black Elk informed Gerald that the Spirits told him they would protect him and he would return home to reclaim his sacred pipe. However, what he went through over there had left scars that could not be seen by our eyes.

"Torrey, tonight we are going to a purification lodge run by a *heyoka wichasa*. In many native communities these sacred men are involved in maintaining the continuity of fertility on the Earth Mother. They are also involved in providing rain for crops, and health and well-being for the tribe. The Lakota heyoka receives his power from the *wakinyan*, 'thunder-beings'. These thunder-beings we believe are a spirit nation. They are not like living beings yet they are a part of Great Spirit. Theirs is the greatest power in the whole universe. It is the power of the hot and cold mixing way above the clouds. It is lightning. It is blue lightning from the sun. When they work it is like atomic power. It is as powerful as the making of another sun. The thunder power protects and destroys. It is good and bad as nature can appear good and bad. It is called the great winged power. We believe that lightning branches out to a good and bad part. The good part is the Light that comes from Great Spirit. It contains what was the first Light on the Earth Mother when no other light existed. There are times when you see lightening coming down in just one streak with no fork at the end. This Light blesses people. This lightening can be another link between Great Spirit and the Earth Mother. The lightening power is awesome . Even Uncle Wallace fears it at times. I know I do. It can have a tremendous destructive aspect. The lightning from the South is always the most dangerous. If it collides with another lightning it can kill you. Only those who have had visions of the thunder-beings of the West can act as heyokas. They have a sacred power and can share it with the people. Uncle Wallace and Red Buffalo both carry this medicine."

Something unusual began to happen to me as we got closer and closer to our destination. It felt like some uncontrollable force took over my tongue and whenever I wanted to say Gerald I said Bill instead. I became completely embarrassed by my apparent lack of consideration for my San Diego kola. The closer we got the more frustrating that word became. He had no idea why I could not say his name. He knew I had stayed in contact with his brother Bill over the years via letters. He knew I had even completed a hanbleycha for Bill after he got quite sick from his ever present diabetes issue a few years back. But he also knew he looked nothing like his brother and it could not be that I had them confused in my mind. It had to seem entirely out of character for me not to be able to say Gerald. I had to really concentrate to squeak out his name. I have never experienced this phenomenon since.

The heat was thick and the dusky sky was filled with fireflies as we finally turned down the dirt road leading to Johnny's house. In the now dimming light I could see a small rectangular structure with weather-beaten siding and warped wooden steps leading up to the front door. As we approached slowly giving those in the house a chance to prepare further for our arrival a thin shape emerged from the house that I recognized immediately as Bill-Gerald's brother. His wide grin, and twinkling eyes told me he had planned being here as a surprise. Little reminders of the great mystery of my pathway cropped up when I least expected. I told Bill about my language problem and we all roared in laughter. No one had any real explanation. I thought Bill looked frail. I had not seen him since our time spent together several years ago at Wilderness Gardens.

We met Johnny's wife and children who all discreetly disappeared into another room of the tidy residence after we were introduced. His wife explained that her husband was down by the stone-people-lodge starting his preparation. We took note and got ready for the ceremony ourselves retrieving our water bottles and towels out of our car. I noticed the fireflies had gotten thicker. They reminded me of the little lightnings I had experienced inside many ceremonies with Grandfather.

The wild sounds of the insects and animals of the night were reminiscent of a scene out of a Louisiana bayou. I could smell the electricity in the air.

A moment of fear gripped me as I thought about the ceremony that evening. After Bill and I got caught up on personal histories he began to tell me more of what I would be experiencing to put me at ease. Gerald and I listened silently. "A heyoka is an upside down, backward and forward, yes and no, contrary man. Anybody can be made into a heyoka from one day to the next whether he likes it or not. If you have a dream about the lightning and the thunderbirds, when you wake up in the morning there is nothing you can do about it-you are heyoka."

"When the thunderbirds send a dream to a man they appoint him to work their power in a human manner. He doesn't even have to see actual lightning in his dream or hear the thunder. Sometimes they send him a symbol like a horse riding to him with certain riders with grass in their hair and belts. He will know this dream comes from the wakinyan. Then he will have to perform the dream in public to free himself. Some will receive special power. Others must act some shameful aspect of the dream to satisfy the thunder-beings."

"Kola, tonight watch and listen very carefully. I will be singing for our ceremony. When Johnny says 'yes' he will mean 'no'. If he says 'he hates you' it means he really 'likes you'. He will walk backwards. The hotter it gets in our stone-people-lodge the colder Johnny will be. I have seen heyokas sweating profusely in forty degrees below zero." We were walking slowly to the creek bed behind Johnny's property. The lightning shooting across the sky was getting closer by the minute. It grew louder. This was a dry lightning storm. No rain had been predicted.

I could see him clearly in the light reflected from the sacred fire already heating up the stones for our ceremony. He was around our age, medium build, smaller than Bill with short cropped black hair. Though he was cordial I could see changes going on with his movements as he sat by the fire. The heyoka mannerisms were kicking in as we each settled down. He had greeted us and then gone into a meditation of his own around the fire. He moved backwards to his sitting position. The lightning strikes that had started many miles away were literally almost over the top of us. The thunder rattled each of us with each flash that lit up the sky as if it were daylight.

Bill was now working the fire. When Johnny stated they were not ready yet we knew it was about time to crawl into the stone-people-lodge. We would be four participants that evening. Johnny went in first and sat in the Southwest. Gerald went in next and sat in the Southeast. I could smell the electricity in the air as I crawled into the Northeast section of the lodge. Bill occupied the

Northwestern space after he brought in the stones for the first door of our ceremony. We completed four doors that evening.

The temperature grew extremely hot. Sweat began to pour out of me almost immediately once our ceremony began within the blanketed and hide covered saplings. It may not have been raining outside but it felt like it was inside. From my view I could see Johnny was cold. He looked to be shivering. Not a trickle of sweat could be seen on his body from the steam that now billowed from the stones he poured water over. It was pleasant to hear Bill's voice sing again the four songs each door. I could smell the rich scent of that wet earth and I once again enjoyed the whisper of the water sizzling and crackling over the stones. I felt strong in spite of the intense heat.

All the movements in the ceremony happened counter-clockwise. These movements were the opposite of what I was used to in our work. In the second round of the lodge it grew so hot Gerald asked to step outside. I had never seen him do this before. I huddled under my towel for protection from the searing steam. I saw Johnny move several stones with his bare hands. We would never do this in our purification ceremonies because it would cause severe burns. I wondered if he had used some of the special herb that heyokas were said to use in their *shunka,* "dog ceremonies". A heyoka is capable of reaching into a boiling pot of water without even receiving so much as a blister to retrieve the meat from the soup. Bill explained to me later that night that the soup was considered very powerful medicine for those in attendance.

Grandfather had explained to me that the heyoka medicine utilized to prevent the burns came from a bluish grey moss. The root of that moss was called *heyoka pejuta.* He said that if a man who was not heyoka tried to perform that ceremony he would be severely burned. It was another reminder of the seriousness of these matters. When the ceremony was over I noticed as I crawled out that the piles of old stones that had not been fired up that night were red hot anyway. They sat in the open ground beyond the lodge at least forty feet away. I had been taught to not ask why about such mysteries. When I shook his hand after the four doors were completed it was cold as ice. Bill translated much of the ceremony for me later that night from the "backwards talk" in Lakota.

As I looked into Johnny's eyes before leaving that evening I imagined he must have been wondering how our two worlds had come together at that moment in time. My tobacco offering to him was given out of great respect just the same. In the view of a shaman, tobacco comes from the earth and rises up to heaven. When the Creator sees it he takes notice. Its a sacred statement. It means that the Creator is being called to witness the interaction.

CHAPTER 25
SHAMANIC EQUILIBRIUM

I realized during the year following my initiation in Egypt that I had morphed from a shaman's apprentice into a neophyte shaman. It had been a steady subtle transformation that was undoubtedly speeded up many light years by the manner in which Black Elk and Red Buffalo shared their expertise. Up until that point in time I felt they could help me out of any difficulties I might create for myself in the worlds that I was now able to move through. That would soon change.

The next phase of my transformation became more arduous and downright dangerous at times. I was forewarned by my teachers that each step I took could become quite precarious. My angel had counseled me, and it seemed my teachers knew it was time to push me out of the nest to begin to flap my wings and see if I could really fly on my own. It is a movement every shaman has to make and I would be no different. I seemed to be in a phase of my shamanic process where I had to sacrifice myself to the spiritual forces that I considered my allies. I had to let go of the control that I thought I had and jump into those unknown currents flowing by me then to see if I could survive the swim.

The enormous power of my initiation in Egypt left me in a struggle for balance in my ordinary life. Little things became incredibly challenging in light of what had occurred over there. The more mundane the less likely I was going to be able to handle whatever came up during that stretch of time very easily. I was attempting to walk in both worlds and neither seemed to be quite in synchronization. I was incredibly fortunate to have so much support from my wife and children who were always there to help me find my way. They grounded me in my ordinary world with their love.

However, there were moments when Tom Petty's song "Free-falling", could have been my theme song. I wondered if there was some sort of balancing going on about receiving special knowledge and then facing some dark force out to cause my destruction. It felt like a dangerous shamanic survival test. If I survived the onslaught perhaps then I was worthy of more knowledge?

During my last years as a supervising park ranger, I dealt with: problematic drunks, drug addicts, drug dealers, vicious pit bull dogs, thieves, deviants in all shapes-sizes-gender, arsonists, armed gang members, sex abusers, and even a brain damaged park worker who became our stalker. One evening

I had to rescue one of my rangers at knife point. By the time I signed my deferred retirement papers I was mentally and physically exhausted. In spite of how chaotic that time was for me, I will always be grateful for the opportunities I was given during my employment there.

Black Elk and Red Buffalo each showed up to do one final teaching stone-people-lodge with me before I left. They each seemed to be trying to give me encouragement. They expressed sentiment to the effect that now was the time for me to overcome my fear of the unknown and walk in my power.

Red Buffalo voiced to me that this might be his last personal teaching with me. They each expressed that my spirit helpers would take over more and more of those duties. Red Buffalo shared these words with me prior to his leaving to go back to South Dakota, "A wichasa wakan chooses a path with heart and follows it. He sees that life is over altogether too soon to worry about change."

I wondered if he was speaking from his heart regarding the big change he made in his life when he retired as a police officer. Maybe he detected my mixed feeling about leaving. "There comes a time in a wichasa wakan's life when he no longer needs his personal history." I felt he was referring to my identity as a Supervising Park Ranger. "One day you will realize that your former identity was no longer necessary, and there was a reason for you to leave it behind you. The freedom you gain from your decision will allow you to collect your power in many more ways. A sacred man needs to be inaccessible at times. He is able then to avoid exhausting himself where other people's thoughts can have adverse effects on him. He is then able to move swiftly and lightly to the next moment of his work. It is there he must remain fluid and unpredictable to succeed."

In that deep part of ourselves we each realized his teaching time was over. We stood together in this sacred bond of friendship and awareness and wondered if we would see each other again. He had helped facilitate a healing for Joshua's bad eye, and he had been a primary force in my training as a sacred man. He joked with me before he left that that place in the North could still be changed to South Dakota. I gifted him several things including my favorite pair of beaded binoculars. We hugged for several long moments.

We never saw each other again in the physical though I felt his spirit at several of my ceremonies. Though we stayed in contact via telephone regularly for a time, eventually that became quite rare. A family member phoned me after he passed away several years later. When I got the call I was hoping it was him.

My time with Grandfather would stretch a bit further down this unusual trail I had become a part of. I couldn't help but notice how deliberate each of his movements were in our ceremonies. He too seemed at peace with his teaching as he sent me off to my new world.

My identity in parks management was left behind in a past life that grew more distant as the miles on my odometer grew in number. All our worldly possessions were loaded into a rented truck as we worked our way North on the interstate. While the rain fell the day we left I shed a few tears for my former life. I had gone through some kind of shamanic death and was hoping for a resurrection at some point in my future. We settled into a rental house in the central valley of California for a few months to reacquaint our children with their Grandparents and explored the rivers and foothills of the Sierra Nevada through the John Muir country of my youth. From this location we made several forays into the North country of Washington and ended up selecting an artist community and historical fishing village. The schools were excellent and the beauty of the area told us it was where we wanted to raise our boys and live. Eventually we chose a property that was located near the Puget Sound surrounded on three sides by water in the center of a point overlooking an island. The air was clean and the water flowed like a giant river through a traditional fishing-rich passage of waters past a beach we owned with our neighbors. There were giant Douglas firs, alders, madronas, and cedars on our land, and the peace and serenity I needed to continue my own work as a sacred man. One of the first structures added to our home was a stone-people-lodge, positioned under the cedar trees to continue my education in the spirit realms and offer help to friends and family that needed it. Black Bears cavorted deep in the surrounding forests and black-tailed deer meandered through the understory by our new house in plentiful numbers. Bald eagles and red-tailed hawks circled in the skies with a plethora of multi-colored others. Orcas and salmon moved past our land in the Puget Sound in plentiful numbers on special occasions. Our boys loved our new environment and all phases of our lives seemed to flow in synchronicity with the new energies of the moving waters around us. Carol landed a job as a nurse at a local hospital. We discovered sun, forest, animals, flowers, and fruits, of very different melodies than we had experienced before. One paradise was lost and a new paradise was found.

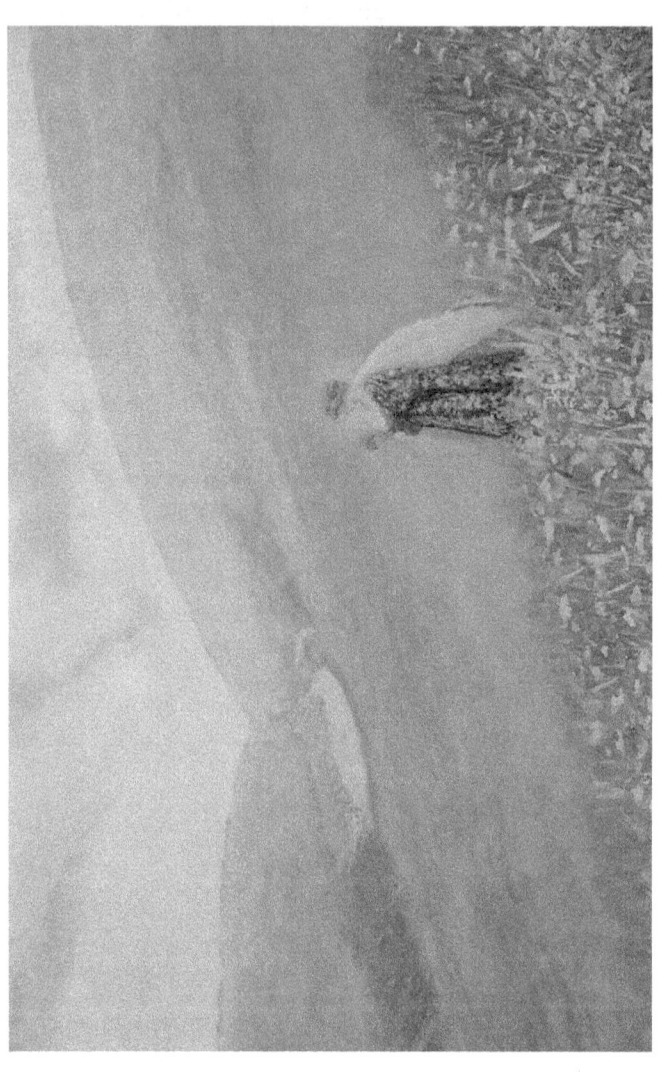

CHAPTER 26
ANGEL DIALOGUE: WASHINGTON STATE

Red Hawk: Why is it necessary for a shaman to go through a period of ordeals?

Angel: Your power increases as you successfully manage each storm. In the calm of the North Country the great mystery will continue to reveal itself to you.

Red Hawk: How do you define the word power and how it relates to my work?

Angel: Power is the demonstration of the active principle of what you refer to as Great Spirit. When you perform a healing ceremony you combine a feeling of gratitude and reverence and confidence to blend your energies in perfect harmony with this principle. Therefore you have manipulated your frequency of vibration and in so doing leave behind any sense of limitation. Every atom, cell, muscle, and organ of your body joins in a union with Great Spirit to accomplish extraordinary focus. By a shamans simple knowing that the possibility exists he gives his power freely to help others. You cannot deplete this power supply. You activate it with your knowing and see it flow in its unlimited form.

Red Hawk: How will I know that my power is increasing?

Angel: You will feel the light that glows within you grow. You will gain confidence and attain successes on your path that will help you measure your progress.

Red Hawk: Some of my ordeals consisted of near death altercations, how has that escape helped me to become a more successful shaman?

Angel: A shaman's work involves facing many life and death situations regarding a patient's health. A successful shaman cannot exhibit any fear or doubt in those moments. The abyss can sometimes await those who fail.

Red Hawk: Did I make the right decision to enter this pathway?

Angel: You have entered upon this sacred trail to be true to your highest aspect. If you have the will to face your own soul you may form a link between yourself and that part of you that is divine.

Red Hawk: What are your thoughts on our selection to make Washington State, our new home to raise our children and continue this work?

Angel: The powers of the universe will always preserve places of seclusion and peace for families like yours. Have confidence in your destiny.

Red Hawk: Should I have safety concerns about my family regarding the path that I have chosen?

Angel: Stand firmly on your chosen ground. Do not resist or resent the circumstances of your life anymore than the plants resent the wind and the rain.

Red Hawk: What advice can I share with humanity from the celestial realm?

Angel: Refuse to hate or kill in a world which insists you must have enemies. Refuse to let fear guide your life. The world is your country. Do not let lines in the sand determine who is your brother or sister. Humankind must invent new ways to avoid wars. Violence begets more violence. When human life is held so sacred that no man dares kill another, then peace will reign supreme again on earth. When greed and selfishness are replaced by generosity and kindness, poverty and disease will disappear from your planet. Love fully, live well, and be free.

CHAPTER 27
ORCA NATION

As spring ripened into summer, my first employment in the Northwest was as a naturalist on an orca research and observation project. My job included piloting a zodiac with four to six project members aboard throughout the San Juan Islands delivering information to them on the whales and other local flora and fauna. Shore birds were abundant in several locations and my background in ornithology served me well in that area of background information. My knowledge of orcas required a good bit of research in order to provide the facts to those who were taking part in the project .

The orca is the one species of cetacean which attracts a fair amount of fear from mankind. This is true even though there are no documented cases of an orca ever attacking a human. Their enormous size, strength, and teeth, certainly get your attention if you are in close proximity to them as I was on many occasions that summer. The three orca pods which numbered around one hundred specimen at the time of my work, live in the Southern Puget Sound from May through October. They are known as the Southern resident orca population by local scientists. They now believe that the decline of wild Chinook salmon runs, global warming, toxic pollution, and heavy vessel noise have been major factors in their decline. Their current numbers fluctuate around eighty orcas. They have been added to the endangered species list.

Orcas are the largest members of the dolphin family weighing about four hundred pounds at birth. Adults can measure more than twenty five feet long weighing more than eight tons with dorsal fins measuring six feet. Some females are known to have lived into their eighties. Orcas are found in every ocean in the world. Next to humans they are the most widely distributed mammals on the planet.

In our region two distinct types of orcas travel the seas; transients and residents. They are distinguished by differences in genetics, language, and food preference. They do not interbreed or socialize. Transients live in small pods up to seven individuals while residents sometimes number over twenty per pod. Transients exist on small mammals such as seals, sea lions, dolphins, and whales, while residents live on fish. I still get excited observing them jump, splash, or spy-hop. They accomplish this by extending their entire bodies out of the water to see what they are able see. I viewed them often using their tails to stun fish and even viewed them push down on commercial fishermen's nets to funnel the fish down to their open mouths. We identified individual orcas by distinct gray swaths on their backs and flanks, as well as the size and shape of their dorsal fins. I took part in a photographic expedition funded by a prominent oceanographic institute to take pictures of malnutrition traits found behind their dorsal fins the following summer. We were issued permits to travel in close proximity to the pods for a short period of time in small Boston Whaler boats. For most boaters it is paramount to stay the legal limit away from them. That limit was one hundred yards in those years, and now that figure is two hundred yards. If they are moving by your boat you should simply shut things down so as not to cause them any problems. I found them to be incredibly intelligent beings.

Our project was staged on some private land on the Northwest side of Orcas Island. Participants set up their tents on the cleared grounds wherever they felt most comfortable. A primitive cooking area with supplies was central to a main fire pit where everyone got to know each other and a camraderie grew each week, until it was time to say our goodbyes and a new group would enter the scene a few days later. Carol and the boys came up as often as possible and I went home between groups.

It was always my feeling that the primary problem with staging a project like this was that it was dependent on finding orcas, and there are times when orcas do not want to be found. Tales amongst local indigenous peoples described stories about the "blackfish" caves that the sacred creatures entered to do their own ceremonies. During one such week we had not seen any orca activity and the participants were incredibly disappointed. The planes that usually spotted the orca by air had not seen a thing. This was the only group of participants that summer that was apparently going to get "skunked". I had been introduced to several members of our group as a practicing shaman by the man who managed the entire operation. They asked if I could help them in any way contact the whales. I let them know I was willing to try to do a ceremony the next day to call the whales to us. I explained I would only take part in this activity if we could not find them in the ordinary manner, and though we covered a wide swath of waters that next morning no sightings of whales were discovered.

That afternoon I explained to them how I envisioned our ceremony taking place on the water. There were four zodiacs with around twenty people total in our group. First, we tied our zodiacs together in a prayer circle approximately one hundred yards off shore. I passed sage and sweet grass to smudge off the people in the boats so as to create as clear a message as possible. I explained there could be no negative thoughts projected to the whales if we expected a successful calling. I filled my Chanunpa asking specifically to see the orca and my sacred pipe was shared by those participating. Our message was clear that we wanted an opportunity to honor the whale nations living in those waters. I finished our sacred ceremony to seal our intent with the honoring song that Grandfather had taught me. It was the same one I sang with him outside the Great Pyramid in Giza to the Earth Conference participants. After the song was over we did a focused meditation and untied the boats. There was no movement on the surface of those waters. For a few minutes we all drifted relatively close together in silence.

Then the most fantastic sounds could be heard in the distance. The orca nation was moving towards us in those waters. I could hear them breathing through their blowholes. I could hear that *pssssh* first. I had heard the whales before I actually saw them. Around the point of the island we were floating by they came to us. It was marvelous and incredibly exciting for each person on the water. There were male bulls, female cows, and their young calves, all moving towards us. Some were seen gliding on the surface of the water and then diving under the sea. Many were gliding by our zodiacs in effortless motion. They came to see who we were. They came in great numbers. Their power and grace seemed effortless. Several orcas spy-hopped in the near distance. These created a rolling movement in our boats. When one of the largest males started tracking directly toward our zodiac many people became a bit nervous by the looks I saw on their faces. We seemed so tiny and defenseless in comparison to the massive shape of his body. He then rolled under our boat raising it in the water ever so gently and looked up at us with a single giant's eye. He seemed as curious about us as we were about him. I was filled with awe. I wondered if being in the middle of a herd of wild elephants could have been any more powerful. I estimated two pods must have come together by the amount of orcas that we saw. What a connection Great Spirit had sent us.

There are moments in a person's life that stand out above others and that list for me seemed to be growing. I got misty eyed as they disappeared into the sea beyond my sight line. The entire group in our boat was pretty choked up with emotion. Had we actually called the whales? The participants were reeling from what had taken place and most realized the magnitude of the gift.

Many were so enamored with that experience they asked if I would lead a stone-people-lodge ceremony for them if one could be found on the island. I explained I would ask my spirit allies for help in that area and see what I could find. The chances of their being a stone-people-lodge large enough for all of them seemed remote. However, a woman who lived near Doe bay was rumored to have one. What began as looking for a needle in a hay stack was narrowed to actually talking to someone who had been in Danielle's stone-people-lodge. That person was willing to arrange a meeting for myself and one of our participants Paul. Paul agreed to be my fireman if we found a lodge to use, even though he had never been in one to that point in his life. The obvious problem became her not knowing who we were. She said she would see us but that her answer would probably be no. I left the matter with Spirit that night.

Apparently those participants were destined to experience a purification lodge. I explained to Danielle that next morning that in ancient times a Chanunpa-carrier would have been allowed to do a ceremony anywhere on Turtle Island, and would have been provided shelter and food as well. She pondered this new information, however, her answer was still in doubt until she revealed that the primary reason she had built the stone-people-lodge was that her life had been spared through an elder sacred man. He had performed a healing on her in the woods in Oregon after she had been stung by hornets so many times she had gone into anaphylactic shock on a back trail at a park she was camped at. Apparently that elder Lakota sacred man had wandered by when her fate was still in jeopardy waiting for medical attention from park staff. She remembers a sucking sound he had done at her lungs and suddenly she was able to breathe again. That elders name was Wallace Black Elk.

Of course when she found out he was my Grandfather and teacher we were not only allowed there but were treated very warmly. The purification ceremony was very powerful. Part of any ceremony I do on short notice with people unfamiliar with this path, includes a teaching session related to prayer-ties, spirit-robes, and other basics to participating. I remind them it is not an endurance test. That it is a special way to pray and connect to Spirit. If they need to exit because of the heat of course they leave the lodge.

The entire group worked several hours before the ritual to clear brush from around the lodge and prepare the dilapidated structure for use. It is a sacred process from preparation to completion.

I am continually reminded of the deep holiness of this sacred walk.

CHAPTER 28
ANGEL DIALOGUE: ORCAS ISLAND, WASHINGTON

Red Hawk: Would you comment on that which I call Great Spirit?

Angel: The creator spirit that many people refer to as God does not have a name that translates into your reality. That is why many refer to that energy as the Great Mystery. You refer to this energy as Great Spirit and that being is described as infinite. Great Spirit exists as a connecting link of Light to all beings. It is the power source behind all that is and the originator of all life. Life returns continuously to this source. After each unit of existence is completed another phase of consciousness begins. It is circle without end.

Great Spirit is the soul of life which pervades all matter including the animal, vegetable, and mineral kingdoms. It is the life force of your world. The soul of man is the conscious part of this divine essence.

Red Hawk: Why do some people hear the voice of Great Spirit and others not?

Angel: Some people never take the time to quiet themselves enough to listen. Practice listening to the voice of Great Spirit and you will be filled with the awareness of many possibilities.

Red Hawk: Is our planet a living organism?

Angel: The earth is a miraculous organism and is very much alive. As your Grandfather's people say nurture the earth and you nurture yourself. Respect the earth and you respect yourself. Love the earth and you love yourself. Poison the earth and you poison yourself.

Red Hawk: How vast is what we call our universe and does Great Spirit flow through it all?

Angel: Your universe is so vast your planet is like a tiny molecule spinning through its space. It is impossible for your consciousness to fully understand how infinite it is. There are infinite galaxies within infinite universes, and infinite forms of beingness that the unnamable one flows through.

Red Hawk: Where do our spirits go when we discard our bodies after living a life on this planet?

Angel: Preparation begins in that unnamable life force you call Great Spirit for your next great adventure within the energy form that is most beneficial to your progression. The soul of man is an eternal Spirit. It comes into your world at birth, not one time but many times, until it progresses to another world fully illumined.

Red Hawk: Would you comment on the word alchemy?

Angel: On your planet, earth, fire, water, air, and spirit, are the essential elements of this creative activity. Each of these elements is utilized in the healing pathway of a shaman-as you know very well. Each of you has the potential to open the channel of complete healing and curing.

Red Hawk: How might I improve my skills as a shaman?

Angel: Focus your mind and your heart with unswerving intent. Keep your body supple for it houses the light that is you. Send your love out into the universe with no strings attached. That action is the most powerful in your realm. Step back from your mind and your heart will help you solve any difficult tasks that you may face. Lead with gentle firmness. Be alert. Treat all life with respect. Be patient. Never inject any thoughts of limitation.

Red Hawk: How can I be certain of right action?

Angel: Right action is often discovered in solitude with an open heart.

Red Hawk: Would you comment on the word desire regarding humanity?

Angel: Human beings must raise their consciousness beyond material distractions and desires in order to attain the highest levels of enlightenment. It is a grave mistake to overvalue your material possessions. They are simply props to be utilized in the experiences you have accepted to be part of your pathway during each life you live. Some lifetimes are full of many props and others hardly any.

EPILOGUE

Of all the mysteries on Mother Earth the Great Pyramid of Egypt stands as one of the most baffling structures in the history of humankind. My time within its walls definitely changed me forever.

Celestial beings were not part of any aspect of my training prior to my Great Pyramid experience. Noted historian of religions Mircea Eliade brings them up as sometimes being a part of a shamans group of spiritual allies or helpers. Mircea Eliade's work with many shamans from diverse cultures is considered some of the most significant ever recorded. That work revealed shamans as invokers, healers, herbalists, oracles, diviners, ecstatic dancers, shape shifters, shamanic journeyers, and more.

Many people have asked me just what is the nature of an angel? Why do they appear to some people and not others? What role do they play in a person's life? These questions are ancient and perhaps the relationship I share with the celestial being I met in the Great Pyramid will shed light on this matter for you.

Some angels have been said to be incredibly powerful throughout history. In the Bible, in Genesis, they are guards with flashing swords. In Ezekiel, they engulf the prophet with awesome visions. In Revelations they do battle with a dragon. My experience would lend credence to the view that they are non-threatening, wise, and loving beings. My angel gave me a song to remember her by and to be utilized when appropriate in my healing work. It is my opinion that anyone who encounters an angel will most assuredly be changed by the experience. They are known to pull back the curtain on the spiritual realm. My angel says that she exists to ease man's arduous journey and to do Great Spirits bidding. She explains that they were created separately, and were given free will, like humans. As for their physical nature she says they assume bodies only as needed to carry out a task.

My work as a sacred man has gone on now for twenty-five years. With the guiding energies of my spiritual allies I have viewed many wonderful results of these practices. These successes have led me to believe that we have only scratched the surface of our physical, mental, and spiritual capabilities. As human beings become willing to go beyond the limitations that we set for ourselves we will realize the power that each of us holds and how connected we are to all life forms.

In the years following my work with orcas in the Puget Sound, I became part of a design team on a seaquarium project outside of Cancun, Mexico, and worked as a consultant on a holistic healing center in the jungle surrounding Chichen Itza, Mexico. Those were some of my most challenging moments as a shaman. While living part time there I developed a special relationship with several wild dolphin pods and found the real Mayan people to be quite extraordinary. Since those projects ended, I have served my local community primarily as a parks commissioner, a teacher, and an artist here in Washington State.

After my move from the backcountry of San Diego to the Northwest I saw less of Grandfather. I relate it now to how an eagle goes about moving its offspring out of the nest until they are finally ready to fly, or die trying. I helped him on several occasions in California, Oregon, and Washington in between work and taking care of my family. Our last road trip together occurred in Australia where we visited Aboriginal shamans and travelled along with Carol and friends to the sacred Aboriginal mountain known to locals as Uluru-Ayers Rock. During this trip we discussed how I would continue on the Sacred Way without his physical assistance. He knew I had to grow and fall down on my own to truly fulfill my own destiny-and so it has been.

Before he passed over in 2004 I had the opportunity to speak with him one last time via telephone. He asked for more photographs from our trip together in Egypt which I gladly sent him. I explained to him I was beginning to write a book about some of our experiences, including what he had taught me, and he said that news made him happy. I could sense the twinkle in his eye even though I had become aware he was very sick. Perhaps he knew all along that our moments would be preserved together in this manner?

His songs and drum-beat echo into the night.

www.ingramcontent.com/pod-product-compliance
Lightning Source LLC
LaVergne TN
LVHW041537070426
835507LV00011B/813